D1274203

THE SCREENPLAY AS LITERATURE

THE SCREENPLAY
AS
LITERATURE

Douglas Garrett Winston

Rutherford • *Madison* • *Teaneck*
Fairleigh Dickinson University Press
London
The Tantivy Press

© 1973 by Associated University Presses
Associated University Presses, Inc.
Cranbury, New Jersey 08512

The Tantivy Press
108 New Bond Street
London W1Y OQX, England

Library of Congress Cataloging in Publication Data

Winston, Douglas Garrett.
    The screenplay as literature.

    Bibliography: p.
    1. Moving-picture plays.   2. Moving-pictures and literature.
I. Title.
PN1996.W555   808.2'3   72-654
ISBN 0-8386-1200-8 (U.S.A.)

PN
1996
.W555

WIDENER COLLEGE
WOLFGRAM
LIBRARY
CHESTER, PA.

160338

DISCARDED
WIDENER UNIVERSITY

SBN 90073070 6 (U.K.)
PRINTED IN THE UNITED STATES OF AMERICA

Acknowledgments

Permission to quote copyrighted material used in this book is gratefully acknowledged as follows:

Jonas Mekas for permission to quote from *Film Culture Magazine*.

For material quoted from *Stream of Consciousness in the Modern Novel*, by Robert Humphrey, University of California Press, 1954. Originally published by the University of California Press; reprinted by permission of The Regents of the University of California.

For material quoted from *What Is Cinema?* by André Bazin, translated by Hugh Gray, University of California Press, 1967. Originally published by the University of California Press; reprinted by permission of The Regents of the University of California.

For material quoted from the book *The Moving Image* by Robert Gessner. Copyright © 1968 by Robert Gessner. Published by E. P. Dutton & Co., Inc. and used with their permission and that of Cassell & Co. Ltd.

Michelangelo Antonioni for permission to quote from his *Screenplays*, The Orion Press, New York, 1963.

For material from *Film Form* by Sergei Eisenstein, translated by Jay Leyda, copyright, 1949, by Harcourt Brace Jovanovich, Inc. and reprinted with their permission.

For material from the book, *The New Wave* edited by Peter Graham copyright © 1968 by Peter Graham. Reprinted by permission of Doubleday & Company, Inc. (for the United States, its territories and dependencies) and Martin Secker & Warburg Limited (for the British Commonwealth including Canada), the book's publishers.

For material from *Four Screenplays of Ingmar Bergman* by Ingmar Bergman. Copyright © 1960, by Ingmar Bergman. Reprinted by permission of Simon and Schuster, Inc. and Lorrimer Publishing Limited.

For material from *Michelangelo Antonioni* by Pierre Leprohon. English translation copyright © 1963, by Simon and Schuster, Inc. Reprinted by permission of the publisher and Georges Borchardt.

For material from *Federico Fellini's Juliet of the Spirits* edited by Tullio Kezich, translated from the Italian by Howard Greenfeld. English translation Copyright © 1965 by Grossman Publishers. Reprinted by permission of Grossman Publishers. For material from the transcription and translation of the final film of *Juliet of the Spirits;* reprinted by permission of Rizzoli Film, the producer of the film.

For material from "Wild Strawberries" by Eugene Archer, © 1959 by The Regents of the University of California. Reprinted from *Film Quarterly,* Volume XIII, Number 1, p. 44, by permission of The Regents.

For material from "The Westerner" by Robert Warshow, reprinted from *The Immediate Experience* by Robert Warshow, Doubleday & Co., Inc., Garden City, New York, 1968, by permission of Paul Warshow.

For material from "Why Neo-realism Failed" by Eric Rhode, *Sight and Sound,* Vol. 30, No. 1 (Winter 1960–61); reprinted by permission of *Sight and Sound.*

Contents

7

Preface

Several years ago, when I first became interested in cinema, it was in those films (most of which were of European origin) that excited me in a way I once thought possible of only the great masterworks of literature. These films—and specifically those of Ingmar Bergman, Federico Fellini, Alain Resnais, Jean-Luc Godard and Michelangelo Antonioni—impressed me particularly with the completeness of their characterizations, the subtleties and nuances of their dialogue, and the complex way in which many of them were constructed. Immediately, I wanted to know more about their genesis, construction and creators; thus I turned to the generally recognized sources of film knowledge: university courses, books, articles, reviews, etc., of that day. I soon found, however, that these were of only limited help. It was not that the instructors, authors and reviewers lacked sincerity, but many of them were so steeped in cinema's past— that of a purely entertainment-oriented medium—or so lacking in an awareness of or exposure to the cultural and literary traditions of the countries where these films were originating that they were unable to grasp adequately the significance of what was going on in cinema at the time. Added to which was the fact that most of these films were slow to arrive upon American shores; when they finally did arrive, it was in only a trickle (not until much later were events such as chronological retrospectives of filmmakers' works more than a rarity). Also, one should not overlook the fact that there was a considerable lag between the time that these films were first shown in this country and the time their screenplays were finally published in English. Unquestionably, the film critics of that day (the early Sixties) were at a handicap when trying to deal with this artistic "explosion" in film (which will partially be the subject of this book); and yet, where they succeeded, they succeeded brilliantly—but amidst a considerable amount of guess-work, vague generalizations and all too frequent excursions into rather obscure metaphysics. In short, there was a great deal of attention given to the "vision," "genius" and "temperament" of the individual filmmakers but not a commensurate amount of attention given to the specific ideas, techniques and innovations that were to be found in the films themselves.

Convinced as I was that so many film masterpieces or near-masterpieces appearing together within such a short period was not simply a fortuitous accident and that these remarkable films were indeed the result of careful preparation and precise design rather than improvisation and chance, and yet still unsatisfied in my desire to learn more about them, I decided to undertake my own study. In this I was greatly aided by the publication in English of several of the scripts for these films; and, of course, repeated viewings of the particular works along with the reading of the all too sparse writings of, and interviews with, the filmmakers themselves also played an important part. Gradually, a specific image began to emerge: that of a new medium whose attempts at increasing its avenues of artistic expression and approaches to reality closely followed the evolutionary pattern of the modern novel.

The rudimentary results of this study were first presented in a course given by me at the New School for Social Research in New York. I have now consolidated all of my researches into the present book, which, I hope, will make what I have personally learned and discovered—or, more precisely, what the filmmakers themselves have learned and discovered—available to more people than would ever be possible for me to reach *via* the classroom.

This book is intended for anyone with an interest in films, and no special knowledge or training is necessary for reading and understanding it; although not intended as an introduction to film, it could well serve that purpose for the uninitiated. I did not plan this work to be a manual of screenplay writing, although those aspiring to that profession may well find it useful, as well as those who hope to become directors or producers.

Finally, I would like gratefully to acknowledge the assistance of two of my students, Barry Levey and Penney Pfaffenback, in the compiling of the bibliography and other details concerning the preparation of the manuscript.

D. G. W.
New York City

Introduction

Twenty-seven years ago, when John Gassner first presented (in a foreword to one of the first volumes of screenplays ever to have been published in the United States[1]) the rather audacious proposition that the "screenplay" could be considered not only as a new form of literature but also as a very important form in its own right, there were more than a few raised eyebrows among the prominent literary critics of the day, who were quick to point out, among other things, the impoverished vocabularies and elliptical sentence structures to be found in these so-called film plays; and, of course, there was the rather obvious fact that most filmscripts were written without any thought toward their possible publication. But wasn't it also true that the number of modern novelists whose writing styles resembled those of scriptwriters was legion (Gassner gave the examples of Ernest Hemingway and John Steinbeck, to mention only a few)? And didn't Shakespeare write exclusively for the stage, and not for publication? Yet the most devastating argument against according literary recognition to the screenplays of that day had nothing to do with their individual merits but instead with the motivation of the writers in question. Did they write for the screen in order to express themselves in a way impossible in any other medium, yet with the same dedication and meticulousness as writers in the more traditional literary arts? Or did they consider their screen-endeavors as mere "hack" assignments, undertaken only to give them the financial support necessary to embark on a real "labor of love," such as writing the great American novel or play? Unfortunately, in the history of the American filmscript, the latter has more often been the case. How many people are familiar with the Hollywood scriptwriting careers of F. Scott Fitzgerald and William Faulkner? And what critic would seriously consider the screen work of these two great American writers in an exhaustive study of their literary accomplishments?*

It is not in the United States, sad to say, but in Europe that we find the first real trend of accomplished writers gravitating to the cinema in order to further their literary careers and not to suspend them. In France, in particular, such well-known literary personages as Jacques Prévert, Jean Cocteau, Marguerite Duras and Alain Robbe-Grillet have all gone on to pursue very distinguished careers in film, not only as scriptwriters but, in some instances, as directors, too.

However, the claim that screenplays are actually literature is based not so much on the recent trend to publish them (along with the fact that many of them do make very good reading), but on the new status that cinema itself has attained—that of an art form. The post-Second World War cinema has proved once and for all that movies can not only entertain people but enlighten them as well, with the same

---

* Contrary to this deplorable trend, Aaron Latham has recently published an exhaustive critical study dealing with Fitzgerald's Hollywood days entitled *Crazy Sundays* (The Viking Press, New York, 1971).

subtleties and complexities that are to be found in any other art or literary form.

The origin of this "flowering" that began to take place in cinema shortly after the Second World War can probably be traced in part (in inspiration) to an article originally published in 1948, in the magazine *Écran Français*, by a French critic who ultimately became a director—Alexandre Astruc. In this article, entitled "La Caméra-Stylo" ("camera-pen"), Astruc first called attention to some of the changes that cinema was undergoing at that time:

> . . . the cinema is quite simply becoming a means of expression, just as all the other arts have been before it, and in particular painting and the novel. After having been successively a fairground attraction, an amusement analogous to boulevard theatre, or a means of preserving the images of an era, it is gradually becoming a language. By language, I mean a form in which and by which an artist can express his thoughts, however abstract they may be, or translate his obsessions exactly as he does in the contemporary essay or novel. That is why I would like to call this new age of cinema the age of *caméra-stylo* . . . By it I mean that the cinema . . . [becomes] a means of writing just as flexible and subtle as written language.[2]

Astruc, in this same article, was quick to see a connection between literature and cinema, in that

> cinema like literature is not so much a particular art as a language which can express any sphere of thought.[3]

And he went on to boldly predict that

> from today onwards, it will be possible for the cinema to produce works which are equivalent, in their profundity and meaning, to the novels of Faulkner and Malraux, to the essays of Sartre and Camus.[4]

However, in order for film to attain the status of literature,

Astruc pointed out, one very important condition would have to be met, namely that

> the scriptwriter directs his own scripts; or rather, that the scriptwriter ceases to exist, for in this kind of filmmaking the distinction between author and director loses all meaning. Direction is no longer a means of illustrating or presenting a scene, but a true act of writing. The filmmaker/author writes with his camera as a writer writes with his pen. . . . how can one possibly distinguish between the man who conceives the work and the man who writes it?[5]

Astruc's call for a "filmmaker/author" was really a reaction against the Hollywood system of production, after which were patterned the film industries in most major countries; for under this system a director's job was merely to follow the script as written by the scriptwriter, both of whom—the director and the writer—were hired by and under the creative control of a third person—the producer—who may also have supervised the film's casting and editing. Astruc's article was instrumental in upgrading the creative role of the director; however, it also had a negative effect in that it contributed greatly to the downgrading of the role of the screenwriter, especially in France. So much was the scriptwriter and scriptwriting neglected in that country, and primarily among those filmmakers associated with the "New Wave" (*nouvelle vague*),* that François Truffaut claims he made *Jules and Jim* (*Jules et Jim*, 1962) "almost as a reaction against slipshod scenarios."[6] Evidently many of Astruc's disciples failed to understand that when he said that the scriptwriter should cease to exist, he did not mean that the

---

* A group of relatively young film-makers who were very active in film production in France during the late Fifties and early Sixties. It is difficult to say whether or not they actually constituted a "school" of film making, but most of them had been film critics beforehand on the influential film journal *Cahiers du Cinéma*. The most prominent names associated with this group are Jean-Luc Godard, François Truffaut, Claude Chabrol and Eric Rohmer (sometimes Alain Resnais's name is included among this group, although he was never a regular contributer to *Cahiers*).

scenario itself should become extinct also, but that the scriptwriting function should be taken over by the director instead.

Before we can proceed further with the question, "Is the screenplay really literature?", we should first determine exactly what cinema is, and, concomitantly, the role of the screenplay and the screenplay-writer in regard to it; also, we must be clear just what the term *literature* should imply, and how it should be used when discussing cinema.

What is cinema?

In this book when we use the term *cinema*, it is to refer to the *creative* process involved in the making of motion pictures or the end results of that creative process. Of course, there are many uses for which motion pictures are employed that do not necessitate any creativity in the making of them, such as the use of motion-picture cameras to photograph bank hold-ups and thus aid in the identification and apprehension of the perpetrators—but we shall not be concerned with such uses in this study. The creative making of motion pictures is often referred to today as *filmmaking;* it consists of not one but several processes, or stages, which are most often designated as writing, directing, and editing (Jean-Luc Godard uses a slightly different terminology; he says that "to make a film is to superimpose three operations: thinking, shooting, editing."[7]) . In the traditional Hollywood methods of production, these three processes were performed in chronological order by three different persons—the writer (or screenwriter) , the director, and the film editor—and, as we have already seen, the supervision and co-ordination of these three tasks was usually the sole responsibility of the producer. However, as Astruc predicted, there is now a trend, especially in Europe, for the writing and directing to be undertaken by one person exclusively, the *filmmaker,* who also supervises—if not performs—the editing himself.

As Godard has pointed out, these three functions often overlap, there being little distinction between the stages which in actuality combine to form one continuous creative process—filmmaking. And not only do these three stages sometimes overlap; they may often occur in varying order. For instance, the most logical sequence for the creation of a film would be as follows: first, the *writing* or *thinking* stage, in which the idea for the film crystallizes, and if the film is to be a narrative or story film, there must be the creation of characters and the fashioning of dialogue—all of which must be given some form or structure; next the *shooting* or *directing* stage, in which the idea, or script, is brought to life through its interaction (or, better still, collision) with the director, actors, scenery, camera, and, ultimately, the photographic film itself; lastly, the results of the shooting—strips of developed film in the form of *shots* or *scenes*—are then assembled, or *edited* (according to some structure or overall pattern), to produce a unified work—the completed film. However, because filmmaking constitutes a single continuous creative process, discoveries are constantly being made during production that usually necessitate many changes, especially in the original idea and/or script. For example, a filmmaker such as Federico Fellini will often make changes in dialogue during—and sometimes after—the shooting because only by being present on the set and hearing the actors speak their lines can he really determine the appropriateness of what may have been written months before. François Truffaut prefers not to give his actors dialogue to memorize but instead to tell them only the gist of what they are supposed to say, which they may then put into their own words. John Cassavetes, on the other hand, has worked in the past almost entirely from improvisation, telling his actors only the situation that they are to dramatize and then making them literally write their own script as the film progresses. It is not only dialogue, but structure and form as well, that may be changed during the latter stages of production. In the making of a documentary the filmmaker may shoot his entire film without even having a point of view; and it may not be until he personally screens all the material he has shot and begins the process of editing that his film will finally begin to manifest itself in a definite form.

Fully cognizant of the fact that filmmaking is really one continuous creative process, we shall, however, in this book devote most of our attention to the first stage—the writing, or scripting. There are two reasons for this emphasis. First, there is the critical importance of this stage in the creation of a successful motion picture—especially of one that aspires to be a work of art. The author has often been told by film-makers how certain films have been created—or, more precisely, *salvaged*—in the cutting room; be that as it may, the author has never personally seen a film in which editing could compensate for, or cover up, the all too prevalent deficiencies of slipshod writing—poorly-drawn characters, weak structures, inane dialogue and fuzzy (or, in some cases, non-existent) thinking. It must always be borne in mind that a film can be no better than the idea from which it has sprung; so that when one filmmaker unabashedly informed the public that in the film that he was about to make "the strongest characters will behave in rather a cowardly way, the most intelligent will talk the most rubbish, and the most lucid will completely delude themselves,"[8] no one should have been surprised at the silly hodge-podge that resulted. The second reason for our concentration on the writing aspect of film-making is that the script, or screenplay, the completion of which usually signals the end of the first stage of a film's production, can aid us immensely in better understanding and appreciating the contributions made during the two final stages—the directing and editing—contributions of which we may be only dimly aware from simply having viewed the completed film.

The author is well aware that his approach is not one which is most in vogue today; it seems that the *visual* approach to film—that cinema is primarily a visual art—is now the most popular among both students and teachers. Although it is undeniably true that film is a visual medium, it is also a narrative one, and contains aspects common to many other kinds of media—film is, above all, an eclectic art.

Another frequently-heard argument is that the cinema should free itself from the restraining influences of drama and literature, and allow itself to find its true form—to the proponents of this argument, a completely visual one. But what these people fail to realize is that literature, drama, or any other art, need not exercise a restraining influence on cinema. Certainly there are some filmmakers who insist on producing works patterned after the Victorian novel; granted that these particular people need to be liberated—but not necessarily from literature. What art form can really claim to be so pure that it has not borrowed considerably from those arts closely allied to it? Certainly not the cinema, nor should it.

The author has also often been told by filmmakers that their works or proposed projects are completely visual and incapable of being thought out or described on paper. Unfortunately, these filmmakers only reveal their ignorance of the allied arts from which they are often knowingly borrowing. It is true that in many instances the idea for a film can only be inadequately expressed on paper—as well it should, for otherwise there would be no reason to make films in the first place. However, to say that something is *inadequately* expressed on paper is not the same as saying that it *cannot* be expressed in that way. Just as no one would claim that reading an orchestral score is as satisfying as hearing it performed, equally no one would claim that a script or synopsis is an adequate substitute for a completed motion picture: both the score and script are only the first steps, albeit very important ones, in the creative acts of music and cinema. Finally, there are the frequent cases of filmmakers who claim that they do not use a script, asserting that they are *filmmakers* and not writers. But he who is unable to recognize when he is writing or thinking during the process of making a film is condemned to make those errors on celluloid (which are more difficult to correct) that would be better made on paper (where they are not only easier to correct but also less costly).

Although in this book we shall not accept the view that film is exclusively a visual art, this does not mean that there will be no discussion at all about this very important aspect; for to consider exclusively the writing side of film-making without regard to the visual elements would be as great an error as to neglect the literary aspects. However, to pursue the visual side of film through the medium of a book presents two very sizable limitations. First, in regard to a full-length feature film, which may consist of several hundred images, to describe each individual image (quite apart from its analysis) would take practically an entire book for only one film.* Secondly, although still photographs from the films discussed here may aid in the understanding of the visual techniques employed—and the stills for this book have been chosen with exactly that purpose in mind— there is, of course, a limitation to the number that can be included in this or any volume; it is hoped, though, that not only will the reader avail himself of the published film-scripts available but also see the film themselves, where possible.

What is literature?

The author realizes that for many lovers of cinema *literature* must be a repugnant word, suggesting something stuffy and precious, not vivid and alive like the films of a Fellini

---

* The reader should note the increasing trend when publishing screen-plays today of including complete shot descriptions of the finished films, and avail himself of the excellent opportunity to study the visual aspects of film-making that these scripts provide.

or Godard. He would hope, however, that the word might suggest not something esoteric and limited, but something universal and limitless instead—the highest level of artistic and intellectual achievement attained by a particular people or culture. And if film should draw heavily on those examples of literature which do seek and, in many instances, do attain such a level of accomplishment, is this any the less desirable, if not more so, than when cinema borrows from such purely entertainment-oriented endeavors as vaudeville, the "dime" novel, or the crime "thriller"? Again, some films are categorized as "literary"—usually in a pejorative sense—which appear to rely heavily on structures or styles or devices that are common to the novel, e.g. narration, rhetoric, interior monologue, symbolism; but are films such as these any more "literary" than those so-called cinematic films that are nothing more than illustrated stories—no matter how visually exciting they may be? As the late André Bazin, the very gifted French film critic, once wrote: "Just as the education of a child derives from imitating the adults around him, so the evolution of the cinema has been influenced by the example of the hallowed arts."[9] The day when cinema—which is barely seventy years old—no longer finds it necessary to borrow from literature will be the day when film equals or surpasses literature as a means of artistic expression. That day is fast approaching.

Methodology of book

The fundamental aim of this book is to better comprehend how the most recent and acclaimed accomplishments of cinema have elevated film to the level of art and/or literature. In pursuing that aim, we shall concentrate, as has already been indicated, on the first stage of the filmmaking process—the writing or thinking stage—as it is embodied in the screenplay, and even in the completed film. However, we shall first have to familiarize ourselves with the language of film—its syntax and structure; all art forms have their own particular grammar and form, and cinema is no different. Because film is also a dramatic medium, we shall need to review those principles of drama that are as equally valid for cinema as for theatre (where they first originated). And since the development of cinema as an art form has been very closely related to the development of the novel, it will also be necessary to examine the similarities and differences between these two very important narrative forms.

Having thoroughly familiarized ourselves with the above topics, we shall then be ready to examine selected screenplays, and the films made from them. Because the contemporary filmmaker has shown an increasing concern for the depiction and/or discovery of reality—whereas the writers and directors of Hollywood's Golden Age* were primarily concerned with myths—the approach taken to or the particular kind of reality dealt with in each of the scripts or films to be discussed in this book will receive a considerable amount of attention; and, concomitantly, we shall also be interested in the unique approach to screenwriting and/or filmmaking that is demonstrated therein. Another paramount concern will be the manner in which each is structured, and according to what kind of logic—dramatic, narrative, or otherwise. Lastly, our study must of necessity be more aesthetic than technical: the quality and validity of a particular writer's or filmmaker's thoughts and ideas must take precedence over his particular mode of expression. Although the dictum "The variations on a theme are more important than the theme itself" may be acceptable for music, it could never be acceptable for film, which, as we shall see, must deal with reality and not abstraction.

---

* Usually taken to mean the years 1930 to 1950.

THE SCREENPLAY AS LITERATURE

1

The Language of Film

Our examination of film and the screenplay must necessarily begin with the language of cinema, which, for our purposes, will consist of two major subdivisions—the syntax, or grammar, and the structure, or form. But before we discuss the specifics concerning this language, we shall need to examine the earliest origins of cinema and see how film rapidly began to develop as an art not long after its inception.*

In our study we shall not be concerned with the controversy over who first developed a successful procedure for both photographing and projecting motion pictures in the mid-1890s—although the preponderance of evidence seems to

---

* In the preparation of this chapter, especially the material dealing with the early development of cinema as an art, I am greatly indebted to Arthur Knight's excellent book on the history of film, *The Liveliest Art* (New York, The New American Library [Mentor] 1957).

point to Thomas A. Edison, at least as to being the first to photograph motion pictures—but what does concern us is that to the earliest pioneers and experimenters in this new medium—notably Thomas Edison in the United States and the Lumière brothers in France—motion pictures were primarily approached as a new type of novelty, whose popularity with the public was sure to be short lived. Among the first filmmakers who both appreciated cinema's potentialities as an art and made important contributions to the development of a film grammar, the names of Méliès, in France, and D. W. Griffith, in the United States, are most prominent. Méliès (who started his career as a stage magician and illusionist) discovered at an early stage cinema's narrative possibilities around the turn of the century; he also introduced the "dissolve," "superimpositions" and other examples of trick photography. It was with D. W. Griffith, however, that the art of film reached its early maturity. Between 1908 and 1912, Griffith made scores of one-reel films (about ten minutes each in length) in which he developed and mastered such important motion picture elements as the camera angle, camera distance (most notably the close-up) and dramatic lighting. Most important, however, was his discovery that by varying the length of a shot* one could affect the psychological response of the audience. While not necessarily an innovator, Griffith single-handedly integrated all previous advances in film technique into a unified art, as is manifestly demonstrated in his two monumental full-length films *The Birth of a Nation* (1915) and *Intolerance* (1916)—two films which remain, even today, giants among cinema classics. By the end of the First World War, the cinema had made some startling achievements and could boast of an impressive body of work (quite remarkable for an art form barely twenty years old). What the cinema did lack, however, was a serious and systematic study of its nature and potentialities.

---

* The basic unit of expression in film; it will be more fully defined later in this chapter.

The first such studies were undertaken in Russia shortly after the October Revolution of 1917, the most fruitful conducted by Lev Kuleshov, a pre-revolutionary fiilmmaker, who became interested in the emotional and psychological effects that could be obtained by the juxtaposition of different images. He and his fellow workers obtained a copy of Griffith's *Intolerance,* which they repeatedly screened in order to analyze its mechanics and structure. Finally, the film itself was physically dissected. The shots and sequences were rearranged, and the effects studied to see how, if at all, they differed from the original structure. Kuleshov's most famous experiment involved an old Russian actor by the name of Mozhukhin. In this experiment Kuleshov employed a close-up in which the actor was perfectly expressionless. This same shot was then juxtaposed to three shots in succession—one which showed a plate of soup; the second, a child playing with a teddy bear; and the third, an old woman lying dead in a coffin. Kuleshov found that audiences shown the experimental shot linkages, praised, surprisingly, what they considered to be the actor's performance—his look of hunger at the soup, his pleasure at seeing the child playing and his grief for the dead woman. From this experiment Kuleshov concluded that it was not the content of the shot alone that determined the emotional response to a film, but the juxtaposition of the images to each other.

Further significant contributions in the formulation of a film grammar were made by another Russian filmmaker, Sergei Eisenstein, who began his artistic career in the Soviet theatre shortly after the Revolution. Eisenstein devised a theory of shot linkage (editing) from his personal studies of Japanese hieroglyphics. He noted that the character for "crying" combines the ones for "eye" and "water," the one for "sorrow" combines "knife" and "heart," and the one for "singing" combined "mouth" and "bird." Eisenstein believed that this form of writing did more than simply coalesce two different concepts; it created, instead, entirely new concepts that were not to be found in the component characters taken alone. Transferring this principle to film, Eisenstein theorized that the shot and *montage* (the linkage of shots) are the two fundamental elements of cinema. He viewed montage, however, as implying more than simply linkage but a "collision" of two factors that gives rise to a dynamic, new concept as well. And, taking a dialectical approach toward art, Eisenstein firmly believed that montage must of necessity incorporate conflict, whether within or between the separate shots. Of almost equal importance to Eisenstein's theory of montage was his discovery that screen time and real time differed: he found that instead of photographing an action or event in one continuous shot, which would reproduce it in its actual time value, he could photograph it from a number of angles in several shots, juxtaposing them together in a slightly overlapping series; this had the effect of destroying real time and prolonging the event on the screen (we shall have occasion to come back to this particular aspect of film editing in a later chapter). Eisenstein's theory of montage, along with his other cinematic discoveries, is clearly demonstrated in his celebrated film *Potemkin* (*Bronenosets Potyomkin*, 1925), and in many of his subsequent works. As may already be apparent, Eisenstein was, above everything else, a theoretician and an intellectual, and besides the extraordinary films that he made, he has left us two excellent collections of essays on cinema, *Film Form* and *Film Sense*—basic reading for any serious student.

Eisenstein, of course, was not the only contributor to the formulation of a film grammar, and throughout the rest of this book we shall have occasion to consider the contributions of several other filmmakers (along with some of Eisenstein's other important theoretical contributions). For the remainder of this chapter, we shall discuss some of the more basic elements and concepts of film syntax and structure (much of which is common parlance in the motion picture industry).

The Film Grammar

The shot. This is the basic unit, usually comprising a single image, and is effected by a single operation of the motion picture camera, beginning when the camera starts to operate and ending when the camera is no longer engaged for that particular action. Shots vary in a multitude of ways, all of which affect an audience's psychological and emotional reactions to the subject being filmed.

Shot categories. Shots may vary both in their duration on the screen and in the distance of the camera from the subject being photographed. The terms for these distances, beginning with the farthest from the camera, are: *long shot, medium shot, close shot,* and *close-up.* Shots may also vary with the angle of the camera in relation to the subject. Some of the more common terms are *low angle, eye level* and *high angle.* With the first, the camera points up toward the subject; with the second, the level of the camera lens is approximately eye level with the subject; and with the third, the camera points down at the subject, and usually from a considerable height.

Camera movement (i.e. the movement of the camera in relation to the subject being filmed) may also be an important element of the shot. The more common types of camera movement are *panning, trucking, tracking* and *zooming.* In the pan shot, the camera remains on a stationary axis (such as a tripod) and pivots, either following a subject that is in motion or else giving a panoramic view of the scene (hence the derivation of the term). In trucking and tracking shots, instead of the camera's axis remaining stationary, both camera and axis are in motion in relation to the subject, which very often is in motion itself. In the trucking shot, the camera is on a three- or four-wheeled vehicle which can be moved on a flat surface; in the tracking shot, the camera vehicle moves on tracks that have been placed prior to the shooting. (Sometimes the word *traveling* is used interchangeably for *trucking* and *tracking,* since in both cases the camera is traveling in relation to the subject.) The zoom shot is an optical process employing a special lens that gives the illusion of camera movement toward or away from the subject, while, in fact, the camera remains stationary. However, all these effects can be obtained—although somewhat crudely—while the camera is supported solely by the camera operator, and in such cases the shot is sometimes referred to as being *hand-held.*

Shots can also vary significantly in regard to their *composition,* the function of which in film is almost identical to that in painting, theatre and photography—that is, as a means of expressing the feeling and mood of a subject through the elements of color, line, mass and form. These elements can also be employed to convey narrative or story concepts; this use is termed *picturization,* and is also to be found in painting and photography, but it is associated more closely—from the point of view of cinema—with theatrical acting and directing.

The last quality to be considered is *lighting.* In films that are brightly lit, the lighting is referred to as *high key;* while in films that are darkly lit, with much shadow, the lighting is often called *low key.* Now that we have seen how shots can differ qualitatively, let us see how these same shot differences can affect us emotionally and psychologically.

Shot values: emotional and psychological

Before we examine these aspects it should be duly noted that in the vast majority of motion pictures made each year—both documentary and theatrical—the selection of shots is dictated almost entirely by narrative necessity. For example, to film the complete, uninterrupted action of a biblical battle scene, showing two massive armies confronting each other, a long shot would most likely be employed. If a director wanted to show the entire action of a moving subject, he would doubtless choose a traveling shot; and if a small object, such as a letter or a ladies' hand bag, is significant to the development of the plot of a mystery, a close-up would probably be indicated. It should be borne in mind, however, that the quality which makes cinema an art and not just another means of communication is to be found in the effects achieved by selecting shots that serve *more* than simply a narrative function.

Shot length. This can be an important factor when the rhythmic quality of a film is considered. A series of shots of short duration produces a fast tempo, while, conversely, a series of shots of long duration produces a slow tempo.

Camera distance. This can have many varied effects on an audience. A close-up can convey a feeling of intimacy, while an extreme long shot can convey the exhilaration that comes from taking in the wide sweep of a natural landscape from afar. Or (frequently in the films of Michelangelo Antonioni), a feeling of alienation may be conveyed when the subject of a shot appears as a tiny figure (in extreme long shot) against a wide, spacious background.

Camera angle. This also affects the emotional tone of a shot. The eye-level angle is usually employed when there is no desire to affect the emotional value of the shot—a basic, all-purpose neutral camera angle. A low angle can intensify the dramatic and emotional value of a shot; with it, the image appears ominously large, and for this reason it is often used in mysteries for the purpose of heightening suspense. The high-angle shot, on the other hand, has a diminutive effect on its subject, which thereby reduces its dramatic value.

Camera movement. Perhaps the most interesting cinematic effects achieved within a single shot have been those that have been achieved by employing this technique. The traveling shot has the unique ability to draw the audience closer to the subject, making them participants in the story instead of only passive observers. Camera movement also accentuates the content of a shot. For example, a tracking shot through a forest can make the scene seem more lyrical, and a trucking shot in the midst of an upper-class cocktail party can heighten

the appearance of elegance. Also, a traveling shot down a
street that has particular significance in the memory of a
character can contribute to an already existing feeling of
nostalgia. However, it is the personal directorial styles of
certain filmmakers that we have in particular come to associate with camera movement—a factor that has contributed
considerably to the fluid styles of such directors as Alain
Resnais, Federico Fellini and the late Max Ophüls.

Composition, picturization, and *lighting.* The psychological and emotional effects of these elements have been extensively studied by those working in painting, photography and
theatre, and although we shall have occasion to refer to these
elements again, I would recommend that those readers de-
siring detailed information on the effects that can be obtained
consult suitable texts on the three aforementioned arts. (It
does not follow, though, that because the psychological and
emotional effects of composition, picturization, and lighting
are almost identical for film as they are for these other arts,
they must be used in exactly the same manner when employed in film.)

Up to this point we have only considered the fundamental
unit in film—the shot—taken alone. Now we shall need to
concern ourselves with how shots are joined together to form
different structural patterns. This linkage, as we noted earlier, is referred to as *montage,* or editing.

Structural patterns

A meaningful arrangement of shots that communicates a
whole action or thought is called a *scene.* It can consist of
only one or any number of shots.

A series of scenes that conveys an important idea or a major
segment of a story is called a *sequence.* It is comparable with
a chapter in a book, an act in a play, or a movement in a
symphony.

Shot linkages and transitions. The shots in a scene are

generally linked together by a *direct cut,* which usually conveys the continuity of an action, with no break in time sequence. However, when the time sequence is broken in the joining of two shots, the linkage is referred to as a *jump cut.* For example, if a shot that showed a man opening a car door and then entering the car is joined to a second shot (from a different angle) of the man completing the action at the exact point (or close to it) where the first shot ended, the two shots would be considered to be linked together by a direct cut. If, however, the second shot showed the man driving off—without first showing him completing the action of entering the car—the two shots would then be considered to be linked together by a jump cut.

Scenes are frequently linked together by a *dissolve,* which is effected by having the end of the first shot slightly overlap the beginning of the next. The dissolve usually signifies a slight break in the temporal continuity of a film and can be compared with the dropping of the curtain in a play momentarily between the scenes of an act. Scenes may also be linked together in counterpoint, frequently referred to as *parallel editing,* or *cross-cutting.* This linkage is generally effected by the intermittent use of direct cuts between two scenes that are supposed to be taking place in different locales but at approximately the same time.

The sequences of a film are most often linked together by *fade-outs* and *fade-ins,* which generally signify a major break in continuity (such as the passage of several days, weeks or months) . In a fade-out the last shot of the outgoing sequence turns to black, and in a fade-in the incoming sequence begins with a totally black image that gradually lightens to full intensity. This type of transition can be likened to the dropping of the curtain between the acts in a play.

Rhythm. We have noted that the duration of the shots in a film can affect the tempo of its rhythm. Also affecting the rhythm of a film are the shot transitions. Just as there are a given number of beats to a measure of music, so can there be a given number of beats in a film sequence. The beats usually occur at the shot transitions, and the accents, if any, on these beats can be affected by the type of shot transitions employed. Thus, a direct cut or especially a jump cut has a harsher accent than a dissolve, which tends to produce a slow, elongated beat.

The Film Structure

Just as merely a knowledge of the rules of English grammar cannot provide us with an adequate understanding of the scheme of a novel written in that language, so it is that a knowledge of film syntax cannot by itself help us understand why a certain filmmaker arranges the shots, scenes and sequences of a film in a particular way.

To understand the structure of a particular example of the French "well-made" play of the Nineteenth century, one has only to be familiar with the conventions and traditions of the theatre of that day; all such plays contained dramatic elements—such as exposition, complication, crisis, climax and resolution—which would not only occur in a precise order but would also fall at exactly the same points in each and every instance. However, in the late Nineteenth century and continuing into the Twentieth, as playwrights such as Ibsen, Shaw and O'Neill became increasingly pre-occupied with the subject matter and content of their plays, and less concerned about the form, there began to emerge a distinction between that structure in a play which corresponded to the structure of the "well-made" play (called the "external" structure) and that structure which seemed to derive from the subject matter itself and the author's attitude toward that subject matter (termed the "internal" structure) . Most of the time in today's theatre these two types of structure work harmoniously, and we are not aware of their existence. Occasionally, however, the external and internal structures will work against each other to the detriment of the play; but what is more common, on the other hand, is for the internal structure to completely dominate the external one, if not replace it altogether.*

In the contemporary cinema, and especially in regard to those films that are generally considered to have attained the level of art and literature, analysis of structure can provide us with only a limited amount of insight into the nature of any particular film, because the present trend seems to be away from rigid structures dictated by convention—the way a film is put together being determined more by the intuitive grasp of the filmmaker than by anything else. Thus, the most fruitful approach to structure would appear to be one that attempts to discern both what is the attitude of the filmmaker toward his subject matter and what have been the influences on him in the forming of it. That is not to say that a filmmaker may not be consciously aware of structure, and that he may not deliberately employ both an external and internal structure in his film; but if he does so, his choice or choices are almost certainly determined by his point of view, and not convention.

Notwithstanding the fact that film structure may be to a large measure intuitive, there are still some useful observations that we can make about it. The following is a brief description of some of the more common structures found in film, and their origins.

Direct physical continuity. This is the simplest and most basic form of film structure. It includes the rudimentary elements of the narrative, with events being related in time sequence, and usually shows an action, event or story as having a beginning, a middle and an end. Very often direct physical continuity serves as the external structure of a film.

Plot. Closely related to direct physical continuity, plot consists of a causally connected and motivated series of events or actions. The "laws" of plot come to us from drama and

---

* For a further and more elaborate discussion of internal and external structure see the chapter entitled "The Film Structure" in Haig P. Manoogian's *The Film-Maker's Art* (New York, Basic Books, Inc., 1966).

literature and embody certain elements and conventions such as exposition, rising action, complication, crisis, and climax. The reader is referred to appropriate books on drama and the novel for detailed studies of plot structure. As was true for direct physical continuity, plot may also serve as the basis for the external structure of a film.

Internal logic. This element is very closely related to, and sometimes even synonymous with, internal structure and may often derive from the point of view of the writer or filmmaker. Thus, if he takes a negative or cynical point of view towards the subject matter, his film may very well be structured to reflect this (e.g. the "black" films of Luis Buñuel). Very frequently a film is structured according to the logic (or illogic) of one of the central characters. For example, the protagonist or protagonists of a film who are criminals may view crime as a game or jest, and the film may be made to depict breaking the law in such a light (e.g. *Bonnie and Clyde,* 1967 and *Butch Cassidy and the Sundance Kid,* 1969). However, this does not mean that a film must necessarily be structured according to the logic of its characters; for in the examples cited above, the filmmakers may not hold the view that crime is a joke, and may instead depict breaking the law as something very serious, if not outright vicious and contemptible, even though the criminals in the film are still portrayed as thinking of themselves as being nothing more than practical jokers.

Increasingly evident in contemporary films are examples of internal logic that derive from philosophy, literature and psychology (e.g. existentialism, stream of consciousness and free association, respectively); and we shall be devoting considerable attention to just such examples when shortly we examine individual films and screenplays.

Style. This element can certainly influence film structure, both internal and external. Styles in drama and films such as comedy, farce and melodrama embody conventions that primarily affect external structure, while naturalism and expressionism are examples of styles which are usually associated with the internal structure of a work.

Music. There is an increasing number of contemporary films that employ structures which are commonly found in music. And then there are some short, experimental films that have been made in which the visual images are made to complement a musical score composed and recorded prior to filming (or, in the case of films made of music festivals, at the time of filming). Also, some filmmakers (e.g. Jean-Luc Godard) have begun to call the sequences in their films "movements"; and, indeed, these so-called movements may be said to alternate between tempos that are *allegro* (faster) and *adagio* or *lento* (slower), just as in music. It seems, however, that the most significant employment of musical structures in cinema is to be found in those films that possess a theme; those techniques that are used to develop themes in music, such as *variation* and *counterpoint,* can easily be adapted to the cinema.

Visual logic. This type of logic is completely non-verbal and is associated with the concept of "pure" cinema; the justification for its use in cinema is based on the premise that because shots, scenes and even sequences may contain visual concepts as well as narrative, verbal or intellectual ones, a film may therefore be structured according to a logic that is purely visual. Thus, such a structure would derive from the shots themselves and might not become apparent until the actual time of shooting or, more frequently, the final editing stages of the film. Although, as has already been stated, a thorough examination of the visual elements of film is beyond the scope of this book, there is one very important point that we should not fail to note about visual logic—that it may sometimes conflict with the internal logic of a film. An interesting example of this—an example concerning the use of color in one of the first films to use the Technicolor process, *Becky Sharp* (1935)—is recounted below by its director, Rouben Mamoulian:

A ball is given in Brussels on the eve of Waterloo, at which Wellington, his officers, and hundreds of civilians are present. A messenger secretly informs Wellington that Napoleon is on the march towards the city. Wellington gives an order which is delivered confidentially to all the officers present. Following this, the news leaks out and starts a panic among the guests. They begin to flee as fast as they can. Now, in terms of realism, the officers, who heard the news first and had an immediate duty to perform, would certainly leave the building first. Yet, visually, colorwise, it would have been wrong. All British uniforms of the period were red. Were I to show these in the first shots and then follow them with less striking, mingled colors of the civilians, I would be decidedly building towards a chromatic anti-climax. So I went against plausibility and reason, and based this montage purely on color-dynamics, believing that the rising excitement of just the colors themselves would affect the audience more strongly than a realistic procedure. I divided all guests into groups according to the hues of their costumes and photographed them, as they were running away, in separate shots; this, in the order of colors in the spectrum, ranging from cold to warm. This resulted in the officers leaving the building last, instead of first. But the color montage, from purples and dark blues to oranges and reds, achieved its emotional purpose of building up to the climax of the officers' scarlet capes in flight.[1]

Most assuredly, this apparent conflict between the visual and narrative elements of film is one of the more crucial problems that cinema must resolve if it is to continue to develop along literary and artistic lines. (Throughout the rest of this book we will encounter examples of how other filmmakers have dealt with similar problems.)

The Film Totality

We have seen how there are several things that can influence the over-all structure of a film. But structure only constitutes the bare bones of a film: it needs to be fleshed out and textured by all of the elements of cinema that we have so far mentioned (e.g. composition, lighting, picturization, montage, tempo, rhythm), and many that we have yet to mention, before it can ever be completed. The logical question that follows is, *who* or *what* determines this end product, or *film totality?* The answer is varied and often depends on the purpose of a particular film. First, however, let us look at an allied art, theatre, and see how totality is determined there.

In traditional play directing, the director determines the over-all structure of the play by studying the script, forming at the same time, in his mind's-eye, an image of the play's totality, or how it will look and sound when performed; from that point on, the theatrical director makes sure that all the elements of the play, from the acting to the stage lighting and costumes, conform to and reinforce his personal vision.

Looking at the television film, however, we find a considerably different approach. In this type of film, due to the very limited budgets available, the writer, not the director, is the main creative force. In this situation, the scriptwriter, before he begins writing, decides upon a structure and visualizes the proposed film's totality, incorporating both as he writes the script. Thus, the completed script serves not merely as a blueprint for the film but a step by step series of directions to be followed scrupulously by director, actors and technicians alike. The directors of such films, therefore, have little creative or interpretative function whatsoever, but merely act as general supervisors who see to it that everyone involved in the production strictly follows the script—any deviation from which will surely result in the production falling behind schedule and exceeding its budget.

In the Hollywood feature film we see a mixture of both the stage and the television approaches to determining artistic totality. Because the budgets of these films are usually considerable, and the shooting schedules not as rigid as those in television, more leeway is given to the director in fashioning the finished product. Though the typical Hollywood script is very detailed, the director may often deviate from it slightly. In the past, however, Hollywood directors (who have come by and large from the theatre) have preferred to save most of their interpretative energies for working with the actors, leaving a great deal of discretion in the determination of the film's visual make-up to the cameraman and film editor—a practice, by the way, that is rapidly being abandoned.

In the European film, as we have already mentioned, the write-director has become the paramount creative force. And with this new breed of filmmaker, there is a certain tendency towards pure cinema, towards having the shots themselves determine the film's over-all structure and totality, instead of *vice versa* as in Hollywood. Michelangelo Antonioni is an example of a European director who tries to mediate between these two approaches (i.e. Hollywood *versus* pure cinema) ; for him the script serves merely as a set of mental notes to be improvised from or improved upon at the actual time of shooting. Below, Antonioni gives us some insight into his particular method of directing in this explanation of why he made certain changes in one of the scenes from his film *L'Eclisse* (1962) :

> Why did I change it? Why, because when the scene was composed [written] we had no idea what Piero's house would have been like, so that the screenplay was of value to me only as a psychological note. And even then, only to a certain point. . . . The changes were suggested to me by the actual circumstances at the time of shooting. It can be seen that I also cut out three lines of dialogue, which are superfluous in the new arrangement of the scene.
>
> As far as I'm concerned, it's only when I press my eye against the camera and begin to move the actors that I get an exact idea of the scene: it's only when I hear dialogue from the actor's mouth itself that I realize whether the lines are correct or not.[2]

From Antonioni's approach, we can clearly see that a film's totality cannot be determined solely by the writer at the time of the script's preparation, nor by the director from simply the reading of it: the creative process in the making of film must be in force right through and even after the shooting. There are two other approaches to the artistic totality of a film that, although not as important as the ones mentioned above, are still worthy of our consideration; they are *improvisation* and the *auteur theory*.

We have already mentioned, in passing, how improvisation has been employed by filmmaker John Cassavetes as a means of literally letting his actors write their own script as the film progresses. In the four films that Cassavetes has made in which he extensively employs this technique—*Shadows* (1959), *Faces* (1968), *Husbands* (1970) and *Minnie and Moskowitz* (1972)—improvisation affects their totalities by allowing the actors, in certain parts, to determine such things as where or when to end a scene, at which point in the scene a climax should occur and just how long it should take to build to that climax.*

The *auteur* theory is derived from certain critical writings of François Truffaut that appeared in *Cahiers du Cinéma* in the Fifties and primarily dealt with *la politique des auteurs* ("the policy of authors"); the genesis of this theory came about partly because Truffaut, along with many of the other critics that wrote for *Cahiers* at that time, was particularly impressed with many of the films that were then coming out of Hollywood. In fact, it would probably not be too extreme to say that Truffaut and his colleagues on *Cahiers* were infatuated with these films; so infatuated, in fact, that they wanted to give the director of them the status of authors. However, this was a little hard to do; for, as we have already seen, the director of a Hollywood film in the past not only seldom wrote his own scripts but also seldom had the privilege of selecting those that he did direct. Also, the films coming out of Hollywood at that time presented another problem to the *Cahiers* writers in that they seldom possessed any content, being by and large repetitions of certain popular

---

* In the case of *Faces* in particular, although a great deal of the film was improvised, Cassavetes worked from a very detailed script—much of which was discarded during the shooting—and extensively edited the results of the filming.

movie *genres,* e.g. the Western, the comedy and the crime thriller.

The *Cahiers* critics were undaunted, however, and devised a method of evaluating directors, the *auteur* theory, which surmounted all of the difficulties cited above. Andrew Sarris (in his brilliant article on the subject[3]) states that this theory consists of three basic premises: first, that the director possesses a minimal amount of technical competence; second, that evidence of the personality of the director is distinguishable in the film ("Over a group of films, a director must exhibit certain recurring characteristics of style which serve as his signature"[4]) ; and third—the premise that has the most to do with elevating a film to the level of art and its director to the status of an author—that the film must possess an "interior meaning," which, according to Sarris, "is extrapolated from the tension between a director's personality and his material."[5] Sarris points out that this term ("interior meaning") is somewhat close in meaning to another term frequently employed by French film critics, *mise-en-scène* (meaning anything from, literally, "direction" to—according to Alexandre Astruc—"a means of transforming the world into a spectacle given primarily to oneself"[6]) , but not exactly —both terms being rather indefinable and extremely metaphysical. In short, according to the *auteur* theory, the totality of a film is not really a function of its content, but is, instead, a function of the "collision" of the director's personality with his material—however inferior that material may be.*

---

* There is one very controversial aspect of the *auteur* theory that is really not relevant to our discussion of the different ways in which the totality of a film can be determined; but because it is so commonly associated with this theory it should at least be briefly noted: that aspect is the alleged tendency of the critics on *Cahiers* invariably to praise the films, no matter how inferior, of those directors whom they considered to be *auteurs* and consistently to pan those, no matter how exceptional, of certain directors simply because they did not consider them to be *auteurs;* hence the charge that the *Cahiers* critics engaged in a kind of cult worship.

2

Dramaturgy

In the preceding chapter we saw how certain dramatic elements such as plot and internal logic can influence the overall structure of a film; at this point, perhaps it would be worthwhile to examine more carefully these and other elements that come from drama and see how they are sometimes applied to cinema, beginning first with *theme*.

Theme. This is the thought-provoking idea that pervades the entire production. It is most often simple and profound: e.g. "The apocalypse of our time," "The brotherhood of man," "The dignity of man" and "God's voice (or silence)." The main point to keep in mind about a theme is that its meaning should always be self-evident to the audience—even if only on an unconscious level—not demanding proof or demonstration, but development instead.

A theme is usually present in only the most ambitious films; however, it may also be inherent in certain classic film *genres* (see Chapter Four for such an example—the Western) .

Premise. More common to films than theme, although the two may sometimes be confused. A premise is a proposition that, unlike a theme, must be proved or demonstrated. Some well-known examples of premises are "The sins of the fathers are visited on the sons" (Henrik Ibsen's *Ghosts*) and "Poverty breeds crime" (Sidney Kingsley's *Dead End*) , both from famous plays.

A film may have both a theme and a premise.

Conflict. The counteraction of opposing persons, forces or wills: it is usually considered to be the "stuff" that drama is made of, but, as we shall see, it may or may not be present to any great degree in certain films or screenplays.

Plot. We have already defined plot as a series of causally connected and motivated events. Seemingly a universal element in drama, film and the novel, it may not be a necessary element in cinema, as will be explained in a later chapter.

Crisis, climax, resolution (or dénouement) . Because these entities are so closely related to each other, we shall deal with them together. All are usually associated with and grow out of the plot. The *crisis* is that point in the play or film where the conflict has become so intense that some sort of action must be taken to resolve it. The *climax* is the definitive clash at the end of which one of the opposing forces gains ascendency over the other; it is closely followed by the *resolution,* or *dénouement,* which contains the final outcome and consequences of the conflict.

There is a far more meaningful approach to the concept of "climax" as regards the contemporary cinema, however, and that is to consider it as the point of maximum emotional intensity for a particular film, sequence, scene, or shot. In theatre, this sort of *emotional* climax usually coincides with and derives from the *plot* climax, which is the same as discussed above. In cinema, however, this may or may not be the case, but if the emotional climax significantly precedes the plot climax, there is a danger that the film will appear anti-climactic to the audience. What adds to the complexity of film is the possibility of there being not one or two but several different kinds of climaxes that fall at different points along the progression of a film. Since the contemporary cinema is increasingly concerned with theme, dramatist and scriptwriter John Howard Lawson has emphasized the importance of a *thematic* climax, which he defines as "the fullest expression of the theme."[1] There may also be one for the premise, which would be that point in the film where the premise has been conclusively proved or demonstrated. The most important of all climaxes in cinema, naturally enough, is the visual one: in the previous chapter we saw an example of one type of visual climax—*chromatic;* but it is the *cinematic* climax, the most intense visual moment of an entire film, sequence, scene, or shot, that is by far the most common, but, sadly enough, sometimes the most neglected, in this essentially visual medium.

Unity. This should be found in all films as in all works of art; it implies an aesthetic quality of oneness, of a complete whole. In other words, nothing in the film should be extraneous or foreign: everything should be an integral part of the whole.

Internal (or inner) logic. We have already dealt with this element in the previous chapter, where we saw how it could reflect the logic of the filmmaker himself or one of the central characters. Internal logic, as we have already seen, can play an important role in determining the over-all structure of a film. But it can be equally important in alerting the audience to what to expect; for it must be clear to them that if there are, for example, certain lapses in continuity, these lapses emanate from the character's point of view (if, indeed, this is the case) and not the ineptitude of the writer and/or the director. It is in this respect that the more conventional theatrical styles—e.g. comedy and farce—come into play in alerting an audience to the internal logic of a film. Thus, if an audience understands that the film they are watching is a comedy, they will react differently to a scene in which a man falls off a roof than if they believe the film to be a melodrama.

Characterization. So much has been written on this subject that it is difficult to generalize; however, there are a few definite observations that can be made about this very important but often sadly-neglected aspect of film drama. First, a character must be consistent with his inner logic as presented to the audience. In other words, the actions of the character should not "throw the audience for a loss," although this does not mean that everything a character does has to be anticipated by the audience. Secondly, an audience usually identifies more readily with dynamic characters than with those who are passive, prone to inaction, or are completely negative in their attitudes. Thirdly, characterization should have some basis in reality; after a while, even the James Bond type of super-hero loses its novelty.

Change. This may or may not occur in a film, depending on the inner logic of the characters in the story. The central characters may be emotionally insensitive and incapable of any significant change, or the premise of the film may be that change is an illusion—life goes on as always (we shall encounter such examples, where character change is doubtful, in our discussions of the films *Wild Strawberries* and *8½*). Whether or not change is present, there must always be change in the audience: they, at least, must gain some insight, even if the same insight has eluded the characters themselves.

Foreshadowing. This element can help to prevent contrivance and coincidence from ruining the credibility of a film. Thus, if a character does change, this change should not come as a surprise; and if a last-minute rescue does alter the plot of a film, it too, should be foreshadowed for maximum plausibility.

Movement and progression. These two elements should be present in all films. The audience must feel that either they, the characters, or the film, are moving toward something, e.g. gaining or providing insight; otherwise boredom will generally ensue. (See the definition of *suspense,* below, for a further discussion of these two elements.)

Point of attack. The point at which the film story begins, usually in relation to the lives of the characters. Its selection should never be arbitrary.

Point of focus. A term that is most often used in discussing films from which it is conspicuously absent. When there is no point of focus, the film story becomes diffuse, and the audience becomes disoriented—and this is most often due to the failure of the filmmaker to think through his idea properly and permit it to crystallize completely.

Style. We have already dealt with this element before, but it would be well to remember not to employ more than one style in a single film, otherwise the audience may become confused in its emotional response—that is, not knowing how to react to the film that they are viewing.

Suspense. Referred to here not just in the sense with which it is usually associated (e.g. in murder mysteries), but also in the sense that the audience identifies with the protagonist and is interested in his fate and the outcome of the story. The audience has to be more than just curious: it has to be *concerned* about the outcome if it is really to become involved. Suspense can be a powerful tool, however, in maintaining audience interest, and it is usually the major source of movement and progression in a heavily-plotted film.

Orchestration. Though this term can be applied non-musically to the selection of the shots in a film, it usually refers instead to the selection and employment of the *dramatic* elements—and especially the characters. The principle is that there should be at least some attempt at variation in the selection and use of these elements—and in the instance of the orchestration of the characters, they should not be of the same type or mold. In the Underground film *The Edge* (1967, Robert Kramer), there was such a lack of character orchestration that one critic wrote that not only were all the characters monotonously similar, but that one of the secondary characters looked so much like the protagonist that he kept confusing the two throughout. Later in this book we shall deal with a filmmaker who is a master of character orchestration, Federico Fellini.

Texture. This term refers to the emotional stratification of a film. Is there any variation in the emotional response elicited from the audience to the particular film in question? Is the film fully "fleshed-out"? All these questions relate to "texture."

3

The Narrative in Cinema: Film's Debt to the Novel

In its rather eclectic development as an art, cinema has borrowed extensively from the novel and antecedent literary forms; the inspiration and source for innumerable films, the novel has given to the cinema a literary legacy that we shall have occasion to examine in this and subsequent chapters.

It is not at all surprising from both an artistic and commercial point of view that the cinema has relied so heavily on the novel. Filmmakers, until quite recently, were exclusively the employees of large corporations, for whom they worked under conditions quite dissimilar to those that have produced the great works of world literature. For example, a Hollywood film* may take two to three years to produce

* Frequently throughout the rest of this book, we shall refer to the Hollywood production system as the model after which most other motion-picture production systems around the world have been patterned. The author is well aware that this system, along with Hollywood itself, has for

and involve the collective effort of the practitioners of many different crafts and trades, with the bulk of the time not too infrequently being spent on the pre-production stages (e.g. budgeting, financing, negotiating and casting*) rather than on the creative stages (that is, the writing, directing and editing). This differs considerably from the two or three years of intensive writing that a writer may devote to a novel, let alone the long and, not uncommonly, painful periods in a writer's life that may serve as the basis for his book (e.g. Somerset Maugham's years as a medical student that served as the foundation for "Of Human Bondage," and the innumerable novels based on combat and prisoner-of-war experiences); this should be further contrasted with the admission by the late Ben Hecht, one of Hollywood's most successful screenwriters, that not only did he often undertake two or more films at a time—taking only two days to a week to finish many of his better scripts—but he actually wrote half the screenplay for *Gone with the Wind* (1939) in one week, and without ever having read the novel![1]

Living in the affluent *milieu* that has so often characterized Hollywood, could the filmmaker (i.e. the producer, director and scriptwriter) have been so bold as to believe himself capable of depicting hunger, poverty and war with the same honesty and understanding as someone who had actually lived through such painful and harrowing experiences, and then spent two or three years to reflect and write about them? Would his characters be as real or as believable? A cursory

---

some time now been rapidly breaking down, which in the long run can only be a good thing; however, this apparent breakdown should not detract from the usefulness that the Hollywood production system can have as a model to be deviated from and improved upon. At the least, as we shall soon see, the Hollywood system can give us an insight into why the theatrical motion picture has developed along the particular lines that it has.

* Of course, in the hands of some filmmakers—and, as we shall later see, particularly in the case of Federico Fellini—"casting" can justifiably be considered as a creative function.

examination of Hollywood production over the past fifty years will reveal that, indeed, films were made dealing with every period in history and every conceivable human plight and condition, from famines in China to dust bowls in Oklahoma. The tremendous breadth and the varying success of these films can most certainly be attributed to the inspiration derived from, and the wholesale adaptation of, a wide variety of outstanding novels. So dependent upon and oriented toward the novel has the film industry in the United States become that when successful novelists have been brought out to Hollywood to work as screenwriters, they have been employed primarily to adapt their own novels, or those of other writers, into screenplays, rather than turn out original material for the screen.

For the profit-minded entrepreneurs who run the film industry in America, the novel, and especially the best-selling novel, has always had one very attractive inducement for being made into a motion picture: the characters and story have already been tested on the public, thereby pre-selling the film even before it has been made. Thus, there can be little risk (financially) in turning a best-selling novel into a movie: simply tell the public that the film is even better than the book and a box-office success is almost always assured.* However, as the supply of good novels has dwindled in inverse proportion to the insatiable demands of the film industry, and as screenwriting continues to develop as a viable art in itself, it is the literary qualities of the novel that are becoming more and more evident in contemporary cinema (rather than the novel simply serving as a source to be plundered for its plots and characters).

---

* A rather recent and intriguing variation of this process has been the increasing trend to adapt an original screenplay into a novel and hopefully get it onto the best-seller lists before the motion picture upon which it is based is released to the public—e. g., *Love Story* (1970) and *Summer of '42* (1971).

The Novel's Influence on Film

The single most significant influence of the novel on the development of the art of the cinema is the narrative or story-telling form. The narrative form, however, goes back farther than the appearance of the novel; it can be traced to the very beginnings of Western literature—to the Greek poet Homer, whose consummate story-telling skill is demonstrated in the two great epic poems, *The Iliad* and *The Odyssey*. Concurring on this point, John Gassner has written: "Film narration is akin to epic narration, and if screenwriters should claim Homer as the father of their craft, who shall contradict them?"[2] However, to understand exactly what is meant by the terms "narrative form" and "epic narration," and how they have influenced the development of film, one must contrast both with the emergence and development of drama and the dramatic form.

Dramatic form versus *narrative form*

Drama as first developed by the early Greek playwrights differed from epic poetry in its emphasis on the "acting out" of the incidents in a story instead of only their narration. And, as the Greeks further developed drama, more emphasis was placed on the *conflicts* to be found in the story, along with the *causal* connection between its incidents (as exemplified by the plot), than on the incidents themselves. Greek dramatists next examined the effects of the incidents, or events, on the characters, and, *vice versa,* the influence of the characters on the events. Gradually components such as theme, premise and psychological insight began to appear in Greek drama, and, as a consequence, there was a corresponding decline in the emphasis placed on the elements of the story. Thus, in the earliest narrative and dramatic forms to be found in Western literature, we can see a growing distinction between "story value" (e.g. the inherent interest and aesthetic appeal in the way in which a story is told and what it tells) and "dramatic value" (e.g. the suitability of a story for being acted out, the richness and depth of its characters and the intensity of its conflicts) ; and, as we shall now see, it is significant for the development of cinema as an art that the motion-picture production system that grew up in Hollywood oriented itself toward the former value rather than the latter.

The Hollywood method of selection and developing literary properties

There is no better example of the influence of the narrative form in the development of cinema than the "story department," which is, in one form or another, to be found in almost all the major studios that still exist in Hollywood (in television, the equivalent of the story department is called the "programming department," at least one of which exists at each major network) . The key person in this type of set-up is the story editor, or analyst, whose job is to scout for and study novels, plays, magazines, newspapers and original screenplays for material that he thinks could possibly be the basis for a successful motion picture. If the story editor does find something that appears usable, he will usually "distil" it down into a one paragraph "plot" or "action" theme and/or a one or two page summary, which is then read by one of the producers or executives at the studio. It is at this stage that the fate of most literary properties is decided; for, if the literary property or story idea fails to arouse the interest of a producer in this abbreviated form, it is usually abandoned. If, however, it passes this very important hurdle, a writer may now be assigned to develop it into a thirty to sixty page *treatment,* something that resembles a long short story told in the present tense, which indicates how the writer intends to handle the literary property in film terms and usually details all the action, including some elements of dialogue to suggest just how it will be handled by the writer in the completed script. This last form, which includes all stage and camera directions, is often referred to as the *shooting script*.

The important point to be noted in this brief survey of the stages of development of a literary property in Hollywood is that this method tended to favor story value and narrative form over dramatic value and dramatic form.* The novel, of course, has expanded and explored other areas and techniques (e.g. psychology, symbolism, stream of consciousness) besides the narrative form (and so has film for that matter) ; but it is the novel's emphasis on story, with a looser structuring of events in contrast to the tighter, more structured elements of plot and conflict that are to be found in drama that has had the greatest influence on the development of cinema as an art.†

Some Differences between Novel and Film

So important has the novel been to the development of the cinema that it would be well worth our examining some of the fundamental differences between these two mediums of expression. Of course, besides the obvious differences be-

---

* I must again re-iterate that the above description of the Hollywood production system, in the light of the many changes that are now going on within the industry, is only an abstraction, and I doubt that any major studio actually follows completely this pattern for the development of a literary property; at least none of the ones that I have worked for did. But, again, our major concern here is with the way this system, or vestiges of it, has influenced the development of cinema.

† One does not have to look to the narrative form and the establishment of the story department to uncover the influence of the novel on the development of film; one can go back to before the inception of the Hollywood system, to D. W. Griffith, who, according to Sergei Eisenstein, found the inspiration and ideas for many of his cinematic discoveries and techniques in the novels of Charles Dickens (see Sergei Eisenstein's "Dickens, Griffith, and the Film Today," *Film Form*, trans. by Jay Leyda [Cleveland and New York, The World Publishing Company (Meridian) 1957] pp. 195–255) .

tween the two (such as the reliance on printed words as opposed to images and sound) , there are some very important distinctions in the area of perceptual psychology. First, a novel is generally read by a reader, who is usually alone, at more than one sitting; in other words, the emotional contact of the reader to what he is reading is discontinuous and may take place intermittently over a period of days, weeks or even months. On the other hand, a film is viewed by the film-goer at one sitting, and usually as part of an audience (thereby bringing in certain elements of group response) . Under these circumstances, the emotional contact of the film-goer to the film he is viewing is continuous, thereby making it easier for the filmmaker to manipulate the emotional response of his audience than it is for the novelist to manipulate the reactions of his readers (in this one respect only, however) . Secondly, because a motion picture is usually seen at only one sitting, with the rate of perception controlled by the projectionist and not the viewer, a motion-picture audience generally cannot digest and absorb as much as the reader of a novel, who may go back over any part he is reading and adjust his reading speed to the difficulty of the passages.* Thus, the cinema has tended to favor simpler constructions than has the novel, with considerable effort being expended by most filmmakers—but not all—so that the audience, whose ability to comprehend a film is more limited than their ability to comprehend a book (for the reasons already stated) , is not inadvertently confused. It is partially for these reasons—though it can never be accepted as a justification—that if many films were translated into literature, they would resemble dime novels or, at best, crime thrillers.

Although the analogy to the dime novel may tend to contradict one of the basic premises of this book—that film,

---

* With the imminent widespread introduction of video cassette recorders (which will allow people to view in their own homes films that have been first transcribed on tape) , these two distinctions between film and the novel may eventually disappear.

indeed, can be considered alongside the great works of world literature—we must not fail to take into account the considerable progress that has been made in cinema over the last ten to fifteen years (indeed, it is this very progress that we shall be concerning ourselves with for the remainder of this book). For instance, in 1957 George Bluestone was able to write the following in a very respectable book on cinema, *Novels into Film:*

> The rendition of mental states—memory, dream, imagination—cannot be as adequately represented by film as by language. . . . [Film] cannot show us thought directly. It can show us characters thinking, feeling, and speaking, but it cannot show us their thoughts and feelings.[3]

But, as we shall see, it is the very thing that Bluestone tells us is impossible in the cinema—the rendition of mental states—that filmmakers such as Resnais, Fellini and Antonioni have shown us is possible in this medium, if not more so. In fact, it is in this very respect that the development of the cinema seems to parallel most closely that of the novel: both mediums of expression, in their respective processes of evolution, went from the description and depiction of simple physical events to the description and depiction of events that are of a complex psychological nature.

The metaphor

The Italian film director Pier Paolo Pasolini pinpointed one of the most essential differences between the novel and film when he wrote the following:

> It seems to me the difference between cinema and literature as means of expression can be found in metaphor. Literature is almost exclusively made up of metaphor, whereas in cinema metaphor is almost totally absent.[4]

Pasolini goes on to give an example of how a metaphor might possibly be rendered in film through *montage:*

> In certain *avant-garde* films, the attempt has been made to juxtapose a hyena with Gennarino by joining two frames;* one showing Gennarino grinding his teeth and the other showing an actual hyena with its teeth bared. [Gennarino is the name of one of the lead characters in Pasolini's film *Accattone* (1961).][5]

A similar example can be seen in the British film *Morgan* (1965), in which shots of the protagonist—a lunatic artist who imagines himself to be an ape man—are juxtaposed with shots taken from old *King Kong* and *Tarzan* movies of the Thirties. However, the results of this "metaphorical" type of film editing have been fairly unpredictable, and audiences often find such film metaphors both confusing and sophomoric.† The most that can be said about this type of juxtaposition is that the effects obtained are generally wholly different from those obtained from such in literature. The reason lies in a very fundamental difference between literature (spoken and printed) and cinema—the medium of the filmmaker is direct physical reality, whereas the medium of the writer is the *word,* which serves as a mediating factor between the physical reality that the writer describes and the imagination of the reader, who perceives only a symbol of

---

* A motion-picture camera does not record one continuous image of the subject being photographed, but several separate images, called *frames,* that when projected on a screen give the illusion of motion. Thus, the *frame* is a component of the shot; however Pasolini uses the term here as a loose synonym for "shot."

† This type of metaphorical editing is somewhat related to Eisenstein's theory of *montage,* which we discussed in an earlier chapter—i.e. the juxtaposition of two different images provides a meaning or relationship that was not present in either image taken alone. For examples of how Eisenstein himself attempted to apply his editing principle in a cinematic rendering of the literary metaphor and for an explanation of why he finally abandoned such an approach, see Chapter Eight.

this reality. On this very distinction the Swedish filmmaker Ingmar Bergman has written:

> The written word is read and assimilated by a conscious act of the will in alliance with the intellect; little by little it affects the imagination and the emotions. The process is different with a motion picture. When we experience a film, we consciously prime ourselves for illusion. Putting aside will and intellect, we make way for it in our imagination. The sequence of pictures plays *directly* on our feelings.[6]

This basic but so poorly understood difference between film and literature has been a major stumbling block in the development of the screenplay and cinema itself. For instance it must not be assumed that because it lacks the "metaphor" as the term is commonly used, cinema is therefore impovished and inferior when compared to other literary forms (of course, we are assuming that cinema is, among many other things, a literary form in itself). For, returning once more to the "hyena" metaphor, Pasolini comments,

> Nevertheless, if cinema cannot express directly the metaphor "Gennarino is a hyena," it can still create such an impression in the viewer's mind by forcing the images. If the film-maker wants to represent Gennarino as having the characteristics of a hyena, he can show the image of Gennarino grinding his teeth in such a way that the viewer can form his own mental picture of the corresponding metaphor, i.e. the hyena, or if not exactly a hyena, then perhaps a panther or a jackal.[7]

Not only is cinema in its reliance on an "indirect" metaphor not inferior, but, on the contrary, by its ability to subtly "force" the images in the mind of the viewer, it may well also be superior to other literary forms.* Accordingly, when Pasolini goes on to say that "the stylistic figures of speech which could benefit both cinema and literature, on the other hand, are those which are common to that branch of litera-

---

* Later in the book we shall come across further examples of how other filmmakers have dealt with the problem of the use of metaphor in cinema.

ture classified as juvenile, religious or archaic, and . . . a third art form, namely, music," specifically referring to anaphora (repetition at the beginning of two or more successive clauses or sentences for rhetorical effect) and reiteration,[8] he does not mean that films that employ such stylistic devices should also be classified as "juvenile," etc., but only that the rhetoric appropriate to one medium may not be appropriate to the other.

Novels into Film

The difference between the visual image and the written word, and the failure of filmmakers to be cognizant of it, is particularly clear in the process of adapting novels for the screen. Certainly, many long, sprawling historical novels (e.g. *Gone with the Wind, Ben-Hur,* and *War and Peace*), full of action and rich in colorful descriptions, have been made into successful motion pictures, with no small part of their success being due to color, wide-screen photography and casts of thousands. But when an accomplished Italian director such as Luchino Visconti tries faithfully to adapt a short but exceptional piece of literature, such as Albert Camus's *The Stranger,* the result is a complete failure. Why? For one thing, in a single frame from Visconti's film (made in 1967) there is probably more detail and description of the actual city of Algiers, where the story is supposed to take place (the film was shot on location), than in Camus's whole novel.* In fact, in the novel, *where* the story takes place is not as important as *how* it takes place. But by shooting on

---

* This particular distinction between film and novel has sometimes been referred to as "total visibility," or, in other words, the fact that a filmmaker's camera may unintentionally record details not required for the dramatic development of the film, in contrast to the novel where only those details that the novelist wants to include find their way to the printed page. However, this so-called total visibility of film is not an inherent limitation and can be controlled (as we shall see in a later chapter) by artistic ingenuity.

location, Visconti gave the film a certain documentary quality that was completely alien to Camus's book and which therefore worked against the real intent of the novelist—to depict a man who is completely alienated from life itself. In short, the fact that "a picture is worth a thousand words" may work in favor of the filmmaker in adapting an historical novel; however, in the adaptation of other kinds of literature for film, it may prove to be a disaster. (This was by no means the only problem with Visconti's film, as we shall see below.)

Perhaps something should be said, at least in passing, about Visconti's recent (1971) adaptation of Thomas Mann's novella *Death in Venice*. There has been much controversy over whether or not Visconti's film was faithful to Mann's work, and concomitantly, whether there was any reason for it to be faithful in the first place. My own view is that Visconti incorporated less than ten percent of the Mann novella into his film—and that rather successfully. Whether or not this can be considered a distortion of the original work is a question for a literary purist rather than a film critic. There can be no doubt that Visconti's film works in its own (mostly visual) terms, and this can be attributed as much to the extraordinary depth of Mann's work as to the artistry of the filmmaker.

Before concluding this important topic of novels into film (there shall, however, be more on this particular subject in succeeding chapters), we should concern ourselves with one all too prevalent mistake made by filmmakers engaged in literary adaptations—which is that, when they set out to faithfully adapt a novel into a film, they frequently end up with the plot, characters, setting, and, in some instances, the mood of the book, but rarely its internal rhythm (i.e., the driving force of a novel that derives from its logic). In very long, heavily plotted novels (best-sellers, especially), internal rhythm is of minor importance, and may be absent altogether. But in novels such as Vladimir Nabokov's *Lolita* and Camus's *The Stranger*, internal rhythm is an integral part of their structures; the failure, therefore, to transpose this internal rhythm contributed heavily to the artistic disasters of the corresponding films. (*Lolita* was made into a film in 1962.) In the realm of literary adaptation, it is the ability to transpose the internal rhythm of the work being adapted that is the mark of a truly great film artist; or, as André Bazin put it so well, "The more important and decisive the literary qualities of the work, the more the adaptation disturbs its equilibrium, the more it needs a creative talent to reconstruct it on a new equilibrium not indeed identical with, but the equivalent of, the old one."[9]

Plays into Film

The process of adapting plays into films closely resembles the development of drama from Greek epic poetry, but only in reverse. Thus, it is necessary to restructure material that is in a dramatic form—dramatic in the sense that the main emphasis is on conflict and characters—in a manner that will give it a more narrative form—i.e. with a greater emphasis on the events and the action. This process (which entails a "loosening-up" of the "tight" constructions that are so characteristic of the play form) is often accomplished by expanding the scope and action of the play, adding new characters and, perhaps, introducing a sub-plot (to mention only a few possibilities) . We shall have more to say about the influence of the playscript on the evolution of the screenplay in the following chapter.

4

The Classic American Screenplay

We shall now deal with the best-known and most influential form of the narrative screenplay—the American film script. Having reached its classic form in the late Thirties and early Forties, the American narrative screenplay has continued to be the mainstay of Hollywood—that which has always worked when everything else has failed. (Perhaps a good argument could be made that would attribute the recent decline of Hollywood to deviations from this form.)

The classic American screenplay has come to us as a hybrid of the heritages of both the silent cinema, with its discoveries concerning the nature of cinematic conflict, and the theatrical play script, with its insights into plot structure and character development; this type of film script primarily focuses on conflict, both internal and external, but, above all, it is characterized by conflict that can be expressed visually. This predilection for conflict in the American screenplay has meant that stories have had to be contrived and distorted so that this "all-important" element could be present in each and every Hollywood script. The late Professor Robert Gessner of New York University found the film *Champion*, adapted in 1949 from the Ring Lardner short story of the same title, to be an example of such distortion.[1] In Lardner's story, the central character, a prize-fighter named Midge, is portrayed as a bad kid who grows up to become a "classic" American heel—a character, in this case, totally devoid of any qualities that could remotely be considered as socially redeeming. However, in the screenplay, Midge is given a tailor-made conflict: he is basically a good kid, but is corrupted by his sordid environment—a complete distortion of the Lardner story. It was not enough, however, to simply provide conflict; in the classic American screenplay that conflict, as was mentioned above, had to be presented *visually*, and the film adaptation of John Steinbeck's novel *Of Mice and Men* provides a perfect example of this.

In his examination of the stage and screen adaptations of the Steinbeck book (the screen adaptation was made in 1939), Professor Gessner noted that, in the novel, the inner conflict of George (the ranch hand who is "his brother's keeper" of Lennie, a half-witted brute) is developed almost exclusively by exposition; in the play, on the other hand, George's conflict (whether to "look out" for himself or for Lennie) is developed by dialogue—but dialogue which is much sharper than that in the novel—along with more indirect exposition.[2] However, in the screenplay, Gessner pointed out, George's conflict is developed in an entirely different manner—cinematically—as he explains below:

In the motion-picture script the point of attack is the posse pursuing George and Lennie through the fruit orchard, following Lennie's encounter with "that girl's dress." For plastic impact of flight and chase this opening is more arresting and stimulating; it is an effective cinematic start to the story. For dramatic impact a posse in pursuit visually demonstrates the danger inherent in George's dialectic. As his brother's keeper he is in danger of getting himself lynched.[3]

A close examination of screenplays that were adapted from novels during the Golden Age of Hollywood provides ample evidence of this tendency: to build and sharpen conflict that was often only suggested in the original novel—conflict most often of an internal nature, e.g. a choice the protagonist must make between two conflicting goals, values or women.

Some of Hollywood's most successful films have possessed not only conflict but theme as well; and the huge successes of some of these films can be attributed to the simultaneous occurrence in them of both thematic and plot climaxes—which has the effect of producing one combined cinematic climax. Two such examples are the film adaptations of *Ben-Hur* (made and remade in 1926 and 1959, respectively), whose cinematic climaxes in both cases, according to Professor Gessner, consisted of an "extraordinary chariot race with genuine crack-ups," which "demonstrated perfectly the glory and cruelty of Ancient Rome [the theme of both films]."[4] However, the classic form of the American screenplay can best be demonstrated not in the biblical epic, but in the Western, a *genre* that has survived virtually unchanged even to this day, and has never seemed to lose its popularity.

The Western

As the late Robert Warshow pointed out in his excellent essay on the Western, much of the success of this *genre* can be attributed to "those 'cinematic' elements which have long been understood to give the Western theme its special appropriateness for the movies: the wide expanses of land, the free movement of men on horses."[5] The Western contains many themes, but the most paramount is the imperfectness of the moral code to which the protagonist, a moral man who does "what he has to do," adheres. As Warshow stated, "The Westerner at his best exhibits a moral ambiguity . . . this ambiguity arises from the fact that, whatever his justifications, he is a killer of men."[6] It is from this "moral ambiguity" that the Western hero's inner conflict arises: either to do "what he has to do," that is, to follow his moral code to its furthest extreme, or to renounce the violence that is implicit in it. It is usually the former, however, which he chooses, but often reluctantly.

There is a second theme in the Western film that is of almost equal importance; Warshow described it as the Westerner's desire "only to assert his personal value,"[7] or, in other words, express himself as a man. However, in doing this, the Western hero must necessarily run foul of the society that is rapidly engulfing his frontier world. This society, as represented by its loftier spokesmen—the mayor of the town, the big ranchers and railroad executives, etc.—demands conformity for the sake of expediency, something that the Western hero, because of his nature, is incapable of accepting. And to that segment of society represented by the small ranchers and farmers (who are destined to inherit the West), there is little in the Western hero's struggle for individuality with which they can identify, especially when their own existence is so characterized by confinement and constriction (e.g. having to support themselves and their families by scratching out a living from a barren parcel of land). And, as for the seamier side of Western society (e.g. the saloon-keeper, the gambler, the rapacious store-keeper), a man such as the western hero, with his high moral sense of honesty and justice, can only be an obstacle to its more opportunistic pursuits. In the eyes of this entire society, the only difference between the Western hero and the outlaw—another "individualist," who openly expresses a contempt for society—is that the former can more readily be "used" and exploited. These, then, are the major conflicts of the Western: the "inner" conflict that the Western hero harbors because of the imperfect nature of his moral code (which sanctions violence) and the external conflict due to society's disdain for his desire to express himself fully—both of which arise from the two major themes of the Western. In addition, of course, there is the inevitable confrontation with the outlaw, which evolves out of the plot.

After the hero of the Western has resolved the inner conflict that is due to the ambiguous nature of his moral code and has come to the realization that he must face his adversary in mortal combat (the crisis point of the film), the real drama then becomes, as Warshow pointed out,

> one of self-restraint: the moment of violence must come in its own time and according to its special laws, or else it is value-less. . . . Really, it is not violence at all which is the "point" of the Western movie, but a certain image of man, a style, which expresses itself most clearly in violence.[8]

It is not, however, simply the "style" of the Western hero that is expressed in the violent confrontation with his adversary (which provides the plot climax of all Westerns), but also the complete failure of his moral code (the thematic climax of the film); for the Western hero's victory is really a defeat. Forced to push his moral code to its farthest limits, he is confronted with its absurdity: killing can never serve as the highest value of any system of morality, because it can only lead to further alienation from society (the secondary theme of the Western) and the necessity for more killing.

The Western at its best—like other popular *genres* of the American screenplay—exhibits a high level of sophistication and craft knowledge in the utilization of dialogue, dramatic action, sound effects, music and cinematography. But it is the combining of both plot and thematic climaxes into one explosive cinematic climax that has made the Western such a popular representative of the classic American screenplay even today.

Film Structure in the Classic American Screenplay

We have examined the aspects of plot and theme and have seen how they both are structured in the classic American screenplay; but what about the shots themselves? How are they broken down in these film scripts? André Bazin, in a very influential essay entitled "The Evolution of the Language of Cinema," made some important observations on this very subject.[9] Bazin stated that, in 1938, the way in which shots were broken down was the same in almost every film. And not only was the way that the shots were broken down the same, but also the number of shots in each film varied little (about six hundred). Bazin concluded that the purpose of the shot break-down in the films of this period was twofold: (i) to keep the spatial position of the subject firmly in the mind of the viewer, even when the subject of the shot is spatially isolated (as in a close-up), and (ii) to emphasize the dramatic and psychological ramifications of the action that is being broken down into shots. The camera directions and the break-down of shots in the scripts to which Bazin referred served a purely functional purpose—to allow us to see the action from the best viewpoint and to emphasize those things necessary. Bazin termed this form of shot break-down, or editing, which was to be found especially in American films *ca.* 1938, "analytic." The characteristic technique employed here, Bazin observed, was cross-cutting, or "action-reaction" shots, in which there would first be one of an actor reciting some dialogue, and then a shot of the actor to whom the dialogue was addressed either replying or reacting.

Incorporated in analytical editing are certain philosophical or, perhaps more precisely, metaphysical tendencies that transcend the rather conventional films in which they are to be found. For example, inherent in analytical editing is the implication that the reality of an action can be best represented by showing that action fragment by fragment as opposed to its physical entirety. Also, in the way close-ups and blurred backgrounds are employed in analytical editing, we can very clearly discern a tendency to isolate subjects and objects in space *vis-à-vis* trying to integrate them with their backgrounds. Even in something as innocuous as dialogue cross-cutting, so characteristic of the classic American screenplay, we can see a tendency to interpret all dialogue as an instance of action and reaction between interlocutors rather than interaction. Implicit in analytical editing, as in film editing in general, is the destruction of real time (which, as we have already seen, was a discovery first made by Sergei Eisenstein). However, although editing, or *montage*, may in actuality destroy real time, it can also create its own illusion for the audience—for that is, basically, the very essence of editing.

This analytical approach to the break-down of the shots for a film (*ca.* 1938) did not go unchallenged for very long. In 1941, Orson Welles "shook up" the entire American motion picture industry with his innovative film masterpiece *Citizen Kane.* Two techniques that were perfected in this film specifically negated many of the tenets of analytical editing. One of them was what Bazin termed the *sequence shot*—a scene photographed entirely as one shot, with no editing whatsoever. The second major technique perfected in *Citizen Kane,* and used in conjunction with the sequence shot, has been termed *composition in depth,* or *deep focus* photography. This technique usually permits two separate actions to be photographed simultaneously within the same shot (one in the foreground and one in the background), both actions being dramatically related through spatial composition. The major significance of Welles's employment of these two techniques, according to Bazin, was that this was the first instance in film in which there was shown a respect for the continuity of dramatic space, along with its duration. For example, in composition in depth, instead of isolating a subject in space with perhaps a close-up (as is so often done in analytical editing), the subject is dramatically related to other characters, actions and inanimate objects, all in a single shot through spatial composition. This "spatial," rather than analytical, approach to film that was employed by Welles and other of his contemporaries (such as William Wyler) added to the growing complexity of cinema (whereas analytical editing was ostensibly a means of simplification). Bazin, perhaps not fully appreciating Welles's extensive theatrical background, mistook this new complexity in cinema through spatial composition as the re-introduction of "ambiguity into the structure of the image."[10] But Welles and his contemporaries did not strive for ambiguity in their films: far from it, their approach to cinema was in many ways a return to pure theatre; most of their actor movements and spatial compositions came directly from the theatre—including in-depth compositions, which, in their hands, derived solely from the dramatic exigencies of the plot—as did their reliance on real time and the respect for the continuity of an action. Nonetheless, Orson Welles's challenge to the analytical cinema of his day had a profound influence on filmmaking, both in the United States and abroad, for the next two decades.

5

Neo-Realism and the Nature of Reality

Up to this point, in our study of film and the screenplay, the question of "reality" and its supposed nature has not been an important factor. However, to a vast majority of contemporary filmmakers all over the world, reality is a burning issue and the subject of numerous vituperative manifestoes calling for the establishment of a "new" and more honest cinema. All too often—unfortunately—the calls-to-arms of such filmmakers (or would-be filmmakers) have fallen on deaf ears, and incipient revolutions in cinema have failed to materialize. There was, however, not so long ago, one such movement in cinema that did begin to flower—so-called *neo-realism* which emerged in Italy toward the end of the Second World War.

It may seem a bit ironical that this most important realist movement in cinema should have taken seed in a fascist state in which the film industry was indirectly controlled by the government through nepotism and subsidies, especially when this particular government had such a vital interest in the suppression of the forbidden subject of reality. Surprisingly, though, the cinema in fascist Italy was not blatantly propagandist: the government there seemed content that its national cinema be only escapist and sterile. Characteristic of this escapist cinema in pre-Second World War Italy were the "white-telephone" films—so called because the major portion of their action centered around a white telephone that was located in the heroine's bedroom—and filmed operas. This sterile state of the cinema did not go unheeded; in 1943, Professor Umberto Barbaro of the government film school in Rome (in a manifesto written for the Italian film magazine *Cinema*) called for a new, more vigorous national cinema that he christened "neo-realist." Professor Barbaro's manifesto set forth a four-point program that, Eric Rhode tells us, exhorted the filmmakers of his land to

> get rid of "the naive and mannered clichés which formed the larger part of Italian films"; of "those fantastic and grotesque fabrications which exclude the human point of view"; of historical set-pieces and adaptations from the novel . . . and finally, of the rhetoric which showed Italians in general as "inflamed by the same noble sentiments . . . all of them equally aware of the problems of life."[1]

Even earlier than 1943, however, there had been a hint of what was soon to come in Italian cinema: in 1942, Luchino Visconti had made his exceptional film adaptation of James M. Cain's novel *The Postman Always Rings Twice*. Set in Italy (Cain's novel was set in California) and called *Ossessione*, this film differed markedly from the insipid films of that period, with its sordid plot (adultery and murder) and its use of natural settings. Then, in 1944, as Italian fascism was rapidly crumbling and the Nazis were hurriedly evacuating Rome, Roberto Rossellini clandestinely made the daring *Open City* (*Roma, città aperta*), which chronicled these very events. This film, which used hidden-camera shots of fleeing Germans and real apartments for sets, along with many non-actors, was primarily responsible for catapulting neo-realism upon the cinema of Italy and the world; it was soon followed by the films of many other talented Italians who were also intent on dealing with the grim realities of the war and the immediate post-war period.

It must not be assumed that Italy was the first country to have dealt with reality in its films. For instance, the hardships and uncertainties of life in Germany after the First World War were searingly portrayed in a remarkable series of German films, made in the Twenties, called "street" films, an appellation that derives from such grim titles as *The Street, The Joyless Street, Tragedy of the Street,* and *Asphalt.* And then in France, toward the end of the Thirties, a number of outstanding films were made that reflected the uncertainty and despair of the period just prior to the outbreak of the Second World War (e.g. *Le jour se lève* and *Quai des brumes*).* Last, but not least, reality had even found its way to Hollywood, which has often been contemptuously referred to as a "dream factory." For example, toward the end of the silent era, Hollywood director Josef von Sternberg made a number of films, such as *The Docks of New York* (1928) and *Underworld* (1927), which, as their titles might suggest, dealt specifically with raw, contemporary life, and which were often filmed on authentic locations. However, with the advent of the sound film in 1927, it became necessary to confine most shooting to movie studios owing to the crude and cumbersome equipment then available for recording sound.

Concurrent with the advent of sound and its complete implementation by the major motion picture industries throughout the world—by the end of 1929 most of the major movie theatres in the United States were equipped to show sound—was the beginning of a severe economic depression

---

* André Bazin used the term "poetic realism" to describe French films of this period.

that brought the United States and numerous other countries to the verge of national disaster. Hollywood—which was perhaps the only industry to avoid the financial depression—responded to the times with a concerted effort to foster an escapist cinema—a decision which was richly rewarded at the box office; people did not want to be reminded of the enormity of their plight, at least not when they went to the movies.

The reality of the depression, however, could not be ignored by Hollywood for long, and a number of films were made that dealt with bread lines, crime, corruption and labor violence. (Perhaps the only reason that some of these pictures were made was to capitalize on the bizarre and sensational headlines of crime and corruption that had proven so profitable to many newspaper publishers.) And then, with the entrance of America into the Second World War a few years later, Hollywood once again was impressed with the need for reality in its films; for it found that its own rather glamorous war films had to compete with both actual combat footage that was being sent back from the front lines and the government's own war documentaries. Hollywood resolutely responded with grim and somewhat realistic portrayals of life in combat, e.g. *The Story of G. I. Joe* (1945) and *A Walk in the Sun* (1945). Another important source of realism in Hollywood films was documentary in nature—in 1945, Louis de Rochemont, creator of the popular newsreel series *The March of Time,* made an anti-Nazi spy film, *The House on 92nd Street,* which was a re-enactment of an authentic case from the files of the FBI (the film was actually photographed in the same neighborhood in which the original story occurred). *The House on 92nd Street* started a trend in Hollywood: real backgrounds were now to be used to add a note of authenticity to purely melodramatic films.

Now let us return to Italian neo-realism and ask two important questions: How does it differ from other realistic trends in film? and Why is it important to us today, more than twenty years later? In answer to the first question:

neo-realism differed from other realistic trends in cinema, not so much because of what it accomplished, as we shall soon see, but in what it set out to do and how it went about doing it. As for the second question: the importance of neo-realism today lies in the fact that at this moment, all over the world, young filmmakers are clamoring for a revolt against the sterile and escapist films that are being fostered by the major film industries in their own countries—and, in this respect, the neo-realist experiment that took place in post-war Italy can provide some valuable lessons for would-be revolutionaries in film.

Fortunately for students of cinema, the goals and methodology of Italian neo-realism were clearly articulated by one of its most creative and prolific exponents, scriptwriter Cesare Zavattini. He exhorted the filmmakers in his country to do away with the story and hunt down their material in the streets; to take the simplest of human situations and uncover the elements contained within; to dispose of the professional actor, since "to want one person to play another implies the calculated plot"; and to reject the technical paraphernalia that impedes immediate contact with reality.[2] According to Zavattini, everyday life can never be boring, while drama which tries to impose a plot on "life" is falsification.[3] "Neo-realism desires to interest itself increasingly not with the extraordinary but with the ordinary—with the man who goes to buy a pair of shoes, or who has a useless quarrel with another, or who laughs or cries, as long as the man is a real man and not an actor."[4] That was the legacy of Cesare Zavattini—and neo-realism—to filmmakers all over the world.*
Before we try to assess the success of the Italian neo-realist directors and writers in living up to these very rigorous standards, it would be worth relating neo-realism to the literary antecedents that figured prominently in its development.

Neo-realism was apparently derived from two prominent

---

* It is said that it is Zavattini's most cherished—but yet to be realized—goal to film ninety consecutive minutes in the life of an ordinary man.

movements in European Literature that took place during
the Nineteenth century: Realism and Naturalism. Realism
was a literary movement that sought to emphasize life as it
was actually lived (in contrast to Romanticism) and tended
to concentrate more on character than on story or plot—it
was closely associated with such notable writers as Stendhal,
Balzac and Flaubert. Closely related to Realism, and evolv-
ing from it, was Naturalism. Like Realism, Naturalism also
sought to emphasize life as it was lived, but concentrated,
however, on the more brutal and revolting aspects of human
existence; and, in its desire to be completely objective, it
tended to be devoid of ideals and rather pessimistic too.
Emile Zola, Naturalism's most illustrious proponent, in his
desire for complete objectivity in his work, went so far as to
adopt a "scientific" method of writing; this is clearly reflected in the following excerpt, containing part of what Zola
considered to be the proper methodology for the Naturalistic
writer:

> His first concern will be to collect material, to find out what
> he can about this world he wishes to describe . . . When all
> this material has been gathered, the novel will take place of
> its own accord. All the novelist has to do is to group the facts
> into a logical sequence . . . Interest will no longer be focused
> on the peculiarities of the story: on the contrary, the more
> general and commonplace the story is, the more typical it
> will be.
>   It will take place of its own accord.[5]

It should now be abundantly clear exactly how neo-realism
patterned itself. We can see the similarities between Professor Barbaro's neo-realist manifesto of 1943 and Realism's
concern for portraying life as it was actually lived; the connection between Zavattini's exhortation to filmmakers to
hunt down their material in the street and Zola's instructions
to the Naturalistic writer is unmistakable. There is one important aspect in which neo-realism differed from its literary
antecedents—and that was in its outspoken social conscious-

ness. We shall now pay particular attention to this paramount concern by reviewing some of the more outstanding films to come out of the neo-realist period in Italian cinema.

The most notable film associated with the movement is *The Bicycle Thief (Ladri di biciclette,* 1948), directed by Vittorio De Sica and written by Cesare Zavattini. An unpretentious little film about an unemployed brick-layer in post-war Italy whose bicycle is stolen (without the bicycle the man cannot get a job) and his odyssey in search of both it and the thief, *The Bicycle Thief* employed non-actors for most of the roles—including the principal ones—and was filmed primarily on location. The film shows how the brick-layer meets indifference and even open hostility in his search for the bicycle; and how, at the end, he is subject to total defeat and humiliation when he finally gives up his futile search and attempts to steal one, only to be immediately apprehended—and, what is worse, in front of his small son. Superficially, it would appear that what De Sica and Zavattini have done in *The Bicycle Thief* is to take a "simple" human situation—the film, incidentally, was adapted from a novel—and uncover the elements that are contained within; however, the elements that De Sica and Zavattini seem to have uncovered are those that are usually associated with plot: conflict, crisis and climax—elements that Zavattini himself implied, as we noted earlier, were a falsification of life. Actually, what De Sica and Zavattini have accomplished in this film is the transformation of an ordinary man into an extraordinary one—in other words, a hero—for the brick-layer who is the film's protagonist hunts down the thief who has stolen his bicycle with the same relentless determination one would expect to find in a classic story of revenge, such as *The Count of Monte Cristo,* to mention only one. Is this man, who is not satisfied with merely reporting his loss to the police, typical or atypical? Or is apathy more common than activism—especially among the poor, or lower classes? It may be true that in a way De Sica and Zavattini did take their story from the streets, but it is not so certain whether they did not, in fact, exercise a certain bias in the selection of their subject matter—the same sort of bias that newspapers demonstrate when they publish "news-worthy" and "human interest" stories about the poor.

Pervading the whole of *The Bicycle Thief* is De Sica and Zavattini's concern for the miserable plight of the poor and dispossessed. Their concern, though, remains primarily on an emotional and sentimental level: both the director and writer can feel empathy with the unemployed, but cannot, however, offer any solution to their problems. This inability to think beyond the problems of the individual—and more specifically here, the family unit—and attack the problems of society has been offered as a major criticism of neo-realism. Interestingly enough, this same criticism has been directed at the brief realist period in Hollywood that took place during the Depression, and specifically at the film *The Grapes of Wrath* (1940), adapted from John Steinbeck's novel of the same name. Both the film and Steinbeck's book are concerned with the plight of the Joad family, who are migrant farm workers that make the long trek from the dust bowl in Oklahoma to the grape fields in Southern California, where they hope to find employment and a better way of life. The fate of the Joad family is not a particularly happy one, although there is a note of hopefulness to the ending of the film—albeit somewhat tenuous—that was not in the book.

Steinbeck, like the Italian neo-realists, showed great concern in *The Grapes of Wrath* for the suffering of the poor and down-trodden, and like De Sica and Zavattini he does not present any solutions to their problems—except, perhaps, providing government camps for migrant farm workers, a rather timid proposal, as the government was already providing such facilities, although on a limited basis. John Howard Lawson has suggested that Steinbeck, in "his troubled contemplation of class struggle and his sensitivity to the misery and oppression of the migrant workers . . . moves toward the difficult recognition that the social order must be reorganized. He cannot fully accept this solution, but he is too honest, too deeply involved in the action, to reject it."[6]

It must not be thought that all of the neo-realist film-makers were as muddled in their interpretations as De Sica and Zavattini. For example, Luchino Visconti (mentioned earlier in connection with *Ossessione*), made an extraordinary film in 1947 about the plight of Sicilian fishermen, called *La terra trema* ("The Earth Trembles"), which did propose some kind of solution to the misery of the protagonists. An aristocrat by birth, but thoroughly schooled in Marxist ideology, Visconti had no doubts whatsoever about the implications of his film. In fact, he has said that in *La terra trema* he "was trying to express the whole dramatic theme as a direct outcome of an economic conflict";[7] and right at the beginning of the film Visconti (who himself speaks the narration) tells us that this will be a story concerning the class struggle and exploitation of the working class.*

The film was loosely adapted from a novel (*I malavoglia*) by Giovanni Verga, whose novels of peasant life were influenced by Zola's naturalistic studies of poverty. Shot entirely on location in a small fishing village in Sicily, and using local fishermen and their families for all the roles, *La terra trema* depicts the disintegration of the Valastros, a family of stout-hearted fishermen whose tradition goes back many generations. One of the elder sons, 'Ntoni, exasperated with being exploited by the unscrupulous wholesalers (to whom all the local fishermen are forced to sell their fish), mortgages his family's home in order to purchase a fishing boat and go into business for himself and the entire Valastro family. At first

---

* It is not my intention to imply that Visconti's film is superior to *The Bicycle Thief* simply because he follows a Marxist viewpoint whereas De Sica and Zavattini do not. The point, then, that I wish to make is that Visconti offers *some* kind of solution to the problems he presents while De Sica and Zavattini offer no solutions whatsoever (at the end of this chapter we shall see how Zavattini has answered this particular criticism).

everything goes well for 'Ntoni and his family, and the film seems to be a paean to private capitalism; but fate intervenes and 'Ntoni's boat is lost in a storm. From that point on the fortunes of the Valastro family deteriorate rapidly: the bank dispossesses them of their home, one son goes off presumedly to become a smuggler, a daughter apparently sinks into prostitution and 'Ntoni takes to drink. Finally, with the whole family faced with starvation, 'Ntoni is forced to humble himself and take a job with the wholesalers—whom he despises. The premise of the film, awkwardly articulated by the main protagonist 'Ntoni at the very end—as in so many Visconti films—is that the working class must stick together if it is to throw off the yoke of exploitation: 'Ntoni made the grave error of striking out on his own, of trying to take on the wholesalers by himself—an unequal match and thus doomed to failure.

Visconti, it is true, does offer the exploited a solution—to join together and achieve solidarity. His premise, however, appears far more revolutionary—if that—than the vehicle that he has chosen to pull it along. For although Visconti follows such neo-realist tenets as the use of non-actors and authentic backgrounds, he violates certain others with his traditionally-constructed plot and his highly-stylized manner of direction. Once again we must raise the question of extraordinary *versus* ordinary. For it is quite evident that the protagonist of *La terra trema* is not the typical peasant fisherman: in his relentless determination, his resourcefulness, his sense of dignity, his vision and his leadership qualities, 'Ntoni towers above his fellow men; and, as André Bazin once remarked, even in total defeat Visconti's fishermen still look like Renaissance princes.[8]

Perhaps this would be a good place to examine more closely one of the better known tenets of neo-realism—the use of non-actors. Zavattini's preference for non-actors was originally predicated on his belief that if an audience knows that something is real they will automatically be more inter-

ested in it than if it is contrived. Therefore, Zavattini rea-
soned, if a man is a real man, and not an actor, "He will be
watched up there on the screen with the same anxiety, the
same curiosity which in any public square is sufficient to
excite us upon seeing a handful of people, to run and ask:
'What has happened; what has happened to a real man?' "⁹
Even if we accept Zavattini's logic about the public's preference for reality—which completely contradicts both the tradition and experience of several centuries of theatre—it must
be pointed out that in no instance in all of neo-realism did
real people actually do real things; or, in other words, were
real people used as real people, and not as actors. In *The
Bicycle Thief* and *La terra trema*, non-actors were indeed
asked to act, and, unfortunately, in the worst tradition of
bad acting they did just that. Evidently, Zavattini realized
this, and in a film on which he collaborated in 1953, *Love in
the City (Amore in città)*, he apparently tried to resolve the
problem of the non-actor.

Love in the City was to be the first issue of a so-called film
magazine, and dealt with the subject of love in Rome as
interpreted by six different directors (including Federico
Fellini and Michelangelo Antonioni). In his own episode,
entitled *The Love of a Mother (Storia di Caterina)*, Zavattini wanted to show that there can be no greater love than the
love a mother bears for her child. The vehicle he chose for
proving this premise was based on a newspaper story, which
at the time had shocked all of Italy. Briefly, the story was
as follows:

A young woman in Sicily becomes pregnant out of wedlock.
Dishonored, she is forced to leave her village and come to
Rome, where she gives birth to her child and tries to find a job.
Unable to support herself and her child by either finding work
or getting welfare assistance, she abandons her baby. Anxious
over the fate of her child, the mother goes to the orphanage
where her baby has been taken and makes veiled inquiries;
this move ultimately leads to the disclosure of her true identity

and her subsequent arrest. However, when the newspapers print the story, there is a public uproar, and the mother is reunited with her child and given a job.

For this segment, Zavattini used not only non-actors, but the actual mother in the real case. It was his belief that by having the woman re-create the incidents in the story as they actually happened, a greater sense of reality would be conveyed. Perhaps so, but even in the so-called re-creating of events the woman is still acting, which is all too evident. It is quite possible that the essential difference between the trained actor and the non-actor is that the former is able to do things naturally—that is, without being self-conscious—while the latter is not. When *Love in the City* was made, however, all six directors employed non-actors except Fellini (Zavattini feels that Fellini betrayed the other directors because of this). Today the situation in Italian cinema has been reversed: the use of non-actors is the exception and not the rule.*

There are two other notable neo-realist films that should definitely not be overlooked. In 1951, De Sica and Zavattini made *Umberto D,* a sympathetic study of the problems, both social and psychological, of an aging pensioner. Also in 1951, Giuseppe De Santis directed *Rome Eleven O'Clock (Roma ore undici)* from a script on which Zavattini had collaborated. Based on a tragic story that made headlines in Italy, the film deals with the personal stories (as told in flashbacks) of four women who were killed when a staircase on which they were standing collapsed as they waited to apply for the same secretarial job (along with over 200 other women). Again, however, by emphasizing the extraordinary (or, as in this instance, the sensational) over the ordinary, neo-realism was

---

* The Antonioni sequence in *Love in the City* is also interesting. Taking people who had actually attempted suicide, he asked them to try to re-create the circumstances that led up to their personal crises. The episode itself does not have much merit, but does foreshadow the direction that Antonioni was to go in his later films.

following the lead of Hollywood, which two decades earlier had also discovered that truth was stranger than fiction.

In all fairness to the proponents and practitioners of Italian neo-realism, it must be noted that they were, in fact, aware of many of the criticisms that have been presented here and did, in a way, answer some of them. For instance, regarding the charge that neo-realist films, by and large, offered no solutions to the proglems presented and therefore were often inconclusive, Zavattini replied that of the films that he himself had prepared the screenplays for, "the characters and situations . . . remain unresolved from a practical point of view simply because 'this is reality.' . . . It is not the concern of an artist to propound solutions. It is enough, and quite a lot, I should say, to make an audience feel the need, the urgency, for them."[10] And as for many neo-realist films being heavily plotted, an apparent contradiction of the ideals of neo-realism, Zavattini frankly admitted that films such as *Open City*, *The Bicycle Thief* and *La terra trema* are, in a sense, "metaphorical, because there is still an invented story, not the documentary spirit."[11] Even in a film such as *Umberto D*, which probably came closer than any other neo-realist film in taking a simple human situation and concentrating on the elements within, Zavattini admitted that "the presentation is still traditional."[12] In fact, in 1952 he claimed, "We have not yet reached the centre of neo-realism. Neo-realism today is an army ready to start. . . The soldiers have to go into the attack and win the battle."[13] However, that army was evidently not to see battle; for, by the mid-Fifties neo-realism, which had never been popular with the bulk of Italian movie-goers anyway, was in decline: as post-war conditions improved in Italy, subjects other than the Second World War, unemployment and poverty began to hold a greater interest for filmmakers and the film-going public in that country.

Neo-realism was to influence filmmaking all over the world in many ways (e.g. the use of non-actors, the use of natural settings and the theme of poverty), but, for the purpose of this book, its most important influence on film was that which it exercised on the narrative form as found in the screenplay. In this regard Zavattini has made the following observations concerning the narrative construction of neo-realist films:

> To begin with, while the cinema used to make one situation produce another situation, and another, and another, again and again, and each scene was thought out and immediately related to the next (the natural result of a mistrust of reality), today, when we have thought out a scene, we feel the need to "remain" in it, because the single scene itself can contain so many echoes and reverberations, can even contain all the situations we may need. . . .
> While the cinema used to portray life in its most visible external moments—and a film was usually only a series of situations selected and linked together with varying success—today the neo-realist affirms that each one of these situations, rather than all the external moments, contains in itself enough material for a film.[14]

Before we leave the subject of neo-realism, there is one very important question raised by the experience of this movement that should be mentioned—whether it is possible for a filmmaker to make an authentic film about the poor or working class if he himself has not come from such a background (the Italian neo-realists were, by and large, drawn from the middle and upper classes). When such a filmmaker goes into the streets in search of his material, will he find for us the ordinary or the extraordinary? Will he show us life as it is really lived, or how he thinks it should be lived? The experience of Italian neo-realism in this respect was not particularly encouraging, but that does not mean the question has yet been adequately answered. More experimentation is definitely called for, but the neo-realist experience has at least showed the way.

Neo-realism has left world cinema a rich and fascinating legacy. Its successful assault against official, sterile and escapist cinema has been an important inspiration to film-makers in every country. Its ideas on reality in cinema, such as the use of non-actors and authentic locations and the jettisoning of plot and other dramatic contrivances, have yet to be adequately experimented with, although many (as we shall soon see) have recurred in the works of filmmakers not necessarily associated with this movement. Although it generally failed to transform its social consciousness into social action, neo-realism can be an inspiration to all politi-cally-minded filmmakers no matter what their particular persuasion.

6

Diary of a Country Priest: Robert Bresson and the Literary Adaptation

It would perhaps appear that the film and screenplay that we shall now discuss, Robert Bresson's *Diary of a Country Priest (Le Journal d'un curé de campagne)*, would contradict one of the prime purposes of this book—to consider cinema as a new form of artistic expression—since, superficially, it would seem that the adaptation of the work of another writer or artist (in this case the novel by Georges Bernanos) could never be considered a legitimate aspiration for a serious filmmaker. I could perhaps cite in defense of Bresson, as did André Bazin, the arguments that the history of painting and sculpture is full of adaptations, and that in "the Middle Ages, the great Christian themes are to be found alike in theater, painting, stained-glass windows, and so on."[1]

On my own, I could also add that the ancient Greek play-wrights ransacked the works of Homer and that Shakespeare also relied on sources other than his own imagination for the plots and characters of his plays. But it is not my intention to make a brief for or against the adaptation of literary works into films. Robert Bresson's extraordinary film (which was made in France in 1951) is important not only for what it can tell us about the art of adaptation—which is considerable —but also for what it can tell us about the relationship between those qualities that we have commonly come to associate with cinema—or, more precisely, the relationship between word and image.

Bresson's *Diary of a Country Priest* is an example of a kind of adaptation that is seldom ever attempted in cinema. In most, the writer or filmmaker chooses to ransack the work he is adapting for merely plot and characters. In fact, one scriptwriter, Margaret Kennedy, once wrote that most members of her craft would actually *prefer* to adapt a second-rate, badly-written novel "toward which they have no conscience, but which has some situation or character which has caught their imagination."[2] Not so with Robert Bresson: the novel he chose is an example of first-rate literature; and with it he took few liberties. What is more, when Bresson first undertook this project, he let it be known that he intended to make a completely faithful adaptation of Bernanos's novel, page by page and phrase by phrase. But Bresson is faithful to Bernanos's novel in a very peculiar way; for, as André Bazin pointed out, in Bresson's determination to add nothing to the original—which Bazin saw as "already a subtle form of betrayal by omission"—he "might at least have chosen to sacrifice the more literary parts for the passages of ready-made film material that cried out for visualization."[3] Yet this is exactly what Bresson did not do; and so, Bazin observed, "When you compare the two, it is the film that is literary while the novel teems with visual material."[4] Briefly, what Bresson was attracted to in Bernanos's novel were those qualities that make it great literature, and not necessarily those qualities that would make it easily adaptable for the screen. The question that naturally arises is, How does one render first-rate literature into film? How, for instance, does one represent on the screen such excellent prose as the following (from the novel) :

I realized that youth is blessed—that it is a risk worth running, a risk that is also blessed. And by a presentiment which I cannot explain, I also understood, that I knew that God did not wish me to die without knowing something of that risk—just enough, maybe, for my sacrifice to be complete when the time came.[5]

In Chapter Three we discussed briefly the possibility of finding a cinematic equivalent of the literary metaphor, while also mentioning other figures of speech, such as anaphora and reiteration, which, unlike the former, are readily translated into film. However, in *Diary of a Country Priest* Bresson made no attempt whatsoever to find cinematic equivalents to passages such as the one cited above. On the contrary, passages such as these are rendered almost intact in the screenplay and film. How is this possible? Through the use of a technique called *voice-over*.

Voice-over is an often-employed process in which an off-screen voice accompanies the visual image. Ernest Lindgren notes that there are three distinct ways in which this process is commonly used—commentary, *narratage* and interior monologue.[6] Commentary, Lindgren points out, is essentially employed as an explanatory device, used mostly in informational and educational films where the material being shown on the screen must be accompanied by some kind of verbal explanation in order to be fully comprehended by the audience. *Narratage,* or more commonly *narration,* is a method by which one of the characters is depicted as telling the audience (off-screen) the story of the film. And interior monologue is a form of voice-over in which the thoughts of one of the characters are depicted as if being spoken aloud. An entire chapter will be devoted later in this book to this last form of voice-over, which is sometimes referred to as "stream of consciousness," to see how its depiction does not necessarily have to be accomplished verbally.

In *Diary of a Country Priest,* Bresson employed the second method of voice-over, *narratage,* as his main device for telling the story. However, he used it somewhat differently, in that the reason for the device is not that the narrator (who, in this case, is the main character) is telling us his story long after it has happened, but that he is reading it to us (offscreen) as he writes it in his diary.

Besides fulfilling Bresson's avowed purpose of remaining faithful to Bernanos's text, the voice-over *narratage* in *Diary of a Country Priest* serves another important function: *endistancement,* a term coined by critic John Russell Taylor— which he defines as the employment of "an emotionally neutral commentary on . . . highly charged images which suggest something altogether less cool and classical."[7] We saw in an earlier chapter how the traveling shot is a device that can be used to draw the audience closer to the subject or protagonist, to identify with it or him and allow them to become active participants in the story and not just passive observers. However, this is just the kind of effect that Bresson did not want—that is, for the audience to become active participants; thus, he employs the voice-over *narratage,* which puts a certain distance between the audience and the main character. Why did Bresson feel that this was necessary? Perhaps because, as Taylor points out, he wanted us to be able to judge the protagonist more objectively and to witness the story "with eyes unfogged by too-easy sentimentality."[8] (Of course, we should not fail to mention the rather secondary role that the voice-over plays in the film as a means of linkage and transition between scenes.)

Let us now look at the subject and story of *Diary of a*

Country Priest. As the title would suggest, both the film and the book from which it was adapted are supposedly drawn from the diary of a very simple and humble, young French country priest. In this diary, he faithfully relates his daily trials and tribulations as he tries—although in rather poor health—to be successful in his first parish assignment, and at the same time to lay to rest his self-doubts as to whether or not the priesthood is his true calling in life. John Russell Taylor astutely points out that in the adaptation of Bernanos's book—which is as discursive as one would expect a diary to be—Bresson omits almost everything without a direct bearing on the "understanding and acceptance of his [the protagonist's] role" as a priest: "Every incident in the film, however small and apparently insignificant, contributes in some way to the curé's realization of his own destiny—a destiny in which his illness and his isolation both as a man and as a priest all play a part."⁹

Diary of a Country Priest differs from almost all the screenplays and films that we shall discuss from this point on (except, perhaps, for *Wild Strawberries,* which we shall deal with in the next chapter) in that it is not a film about a plot or a consciousness or a psychology, but a film about a *soul*, about an individual's spiritual life; whereas most of the other films that we shall encounter in this book are about the psychological lives of their characters. Bresson's film is, no doubt, a religious film, but where it differs from the vulgar religious spectacles that Hollywood has manufactured for so many years is in having its spiritual fulfillment depicted with complete simplicity and taste. As John Russell Taylor puts it so well, "Great spiritual dramas are not played out in external action, but in the movement of souls, and this, more vividly than anywhere else in cinema, is what Bresson captures here, in apparently flat, unimpassioned exchanges, while ordinary life goes on all round."¹⁰ Thus, he continues, when the curé recognizes his own true spiritual identity, a dog barks; and when the wife of the local aristo-crat is reconverted by the curé, "a gardener mows the lawn outside."[11]

Now that we have examined both the main narrative tech-nique and subject of Bresson's film, let us move to its struc-ture, which is unique in itself. In this regard André Bazin astutely pointed out that the succession of events in the film

> is not constructed according to the usual laws of dramaturgy under which the passions work towards a soul-satisfying climax. Events do indeed follow one another according to a necessary order, yet within a framework of accidental happenings. Free acts and coincidences are interwoven. Each moment in the film, each set-up, has its own due measure, alike, of freedom and of necessity.[12]

What Bazin is really saying is that Bresson's film has no plot, or at least is not structured according to one.* Thus, when the conflict within the curé is finally resolved—that is, when he finally comes to realize that the priesthood is his true calling in life—this is not the climax of the film; nor is the curé's death from cancer at the end really the termination of the story. Why? Perhaps because of what André Bazin discerned as the film's internal logic: "The pattern of the film's unfolding is not that of tragedy in the usual sense, rather in the sense of the medieval Passion Play, or better still, of the Way of the Cross, each sequence being a station along the road"[13]—and for a spirit, or soul, death is not the end of that road, but only one station along.

I have so far avoided begging the question of whether or not Bresson's stated desire to be faithful to the text of Ber-nanos's novel—and hence his employment of a voice-over *narratage*—is really a legitimate concern for the filmmaker who sets out to adapt a book. In an earlier chapter we saw how it was necessary to first capture the spirit, or essence, of

---

* There will be a fuller discussion of films made from "plotless screen-plays" in Chapter Eleven.

the book under consideration; this may require the establishment or reconstruction of a new equilibrium within the
adapted work, necessitating, perhaps, the search for cinematic equivalents for many of the literary devices to be
found in the original. In short, we saw that an adaptation
was, in most instances, a translation—a translation of literature into cinema. We also saw that in the instance of the
historical novel, which usually contains considerable action
and description, this process of translation presented few
problems to the filmmaker. However, we also saw that in the
case of a superior novel, such as Camus's *The Stranger*, the
translation process proved to be exceedingly difficult. Why?
The reason is simple: *In a great work of literature it is impossible to separate that which the author is describing from
the actual words that he uses.* Thus, the essence of a truly
great novel cannot be extracted from the prose that envelops
it. Here Bresson has discovered something that few other
filmmakers have yet realized—in the adaptation of a significant piece of literature, the reality with which the filmmaker
must work is not the reality that the novelist describes, but
his description of it: *the reality of a superior literary work is
the work itself.* With this in mind, the reason for the failure
of Visconti's adaptation of *The Stranger* becomes all the
more apparent: his error was to believe that the reality of
Camus's novel was in the Algiers that he, Visconti, sought
to record on film and not in the words that Camus used to
describe that enigmatic North African city.*

André Bazin noted that in *Diary of a Country Priest*,
Bresson breaks one of the cardinal rules of cinema "according
to which image and sound should never duplicate one another."[14] But Bazin also added, "The most moving moments
in the film are those in which text and image are saying the
same thing, each however in its own way."[15] In the last analy-

---

* That is not to say Visconti's film did not employ some voice-over
interior monologue from Camus's text; however, the point remains that the
reality which Visconti sought rested somewhere other than in Camus's prose.

sis, Bazin saw Bresson's film as the result of "a dialectic between the cinema and literature."[16] And that is really Bresson's greatest contribution to the development of film as an art: to look on literature, not with mistrust, as something inimical to film, *but as an ally.* Bresson has shown us that word and visual image need not be thought of in terms of equivalency; instead, they may be considered as existing side by side, ready to serve the filmmaker who is astute enough to realize this fundamental aesthetic truth of cinema.

Notwithstanding Bresson's discoveries about and contributions to cinema as an art, *Diary of a Country Priest* can be a very unsatisfying film for most viewers. Bresson's attempt at endistancement can alienate many people who prefer not to view films with detachment but to be drawn into them by a direct appeal to their emotions and sentiments—an approach deliberately eschewed by this director. But here, detachment can hardly be considered a fault; on the contrary, for Bresson it is an artistic necessity.

Invariably those who dislike this film attribute their antipathy to Bresson's use of a voice-over *narratage.* Granted that in *Diary of a Country Priest* this is excessive, its use in this particular film is necessary—and not just for preserving the quality of Bernanos's prose. Although it would be possible to show Bresson's film without this *narratage,* one would only be left with a film about a socially-awkward, pathetic country priest as he plods through his drab, daily routines endeavoring to save souls, and, in the process, perhaps saving his own. Needless to say, this would have little relation to Bernanos's novel. For, as socially awkward as this gentle parish priest is in the book, he certainly is *not* pathetic. The reader of the novel is struck by the curé's remarkable intellect, his complete awareness of his situation and what is happening to him; outwardly he may not be able to cope with certain social situations and the people he must come in contact with in daily life, but inwardly he is totally aware of all these things—of his failings. As the curé says in both the book and film, "But the simplest tasks are by no means the easiest"; yet we would never know that the curé was aware of this without the film's voice-over. Where then is the flaw in Bresson's adaptation? It is hard to say. For one thing, the essence of Bernanos's novel is a spiritual one—and I do not believe that this spirituality is adequately expressed in the film, or at least visually. For example, in the sequence in which the curé sees visions of the Virgin Child just before he loses consciousness because of his illness, the fact is conveyed merely by his voice-over: no hint is given from the images on the screen, which only show the curé stumbling along, trying to keep himself from falling. It is not that I believe that Bresson should have faithfully shown us the visions but that the voice-over itself is totally inadequate, *by itself,* for indicating or expressing this vision.

Much of the difficulty that Bresson encountered in making this film—and much of the film's distinction, too—stems from his sincere attempt to be faithful to the novel. However, in doing so Bresson sometimes lost sight of the fact that film is not only a literary but also a multi-faceted medium, with words (spoken), visual images and music—in this case, words by Georges Bernanos, images by Robert Bresson and music by Jean-Jacques Grünenwald.*

---

* My preparation of this chapter has suffered from the fact that there is at present no published English translation of Bresson's screenplay for *Diary of a Country Priest.* From this point on, if no mention is made in the body of the text whether or not published English editions exist, the reader should check both the notes and bibliography at the back of the book, where all such screenplays, if in existence, are listed.

7

Wild *Strawberries:* A Dream Play

It is only fitting that the first film we shall examine made from an original screenplay should be written and directed by Swedish filmmaker Ingmar Bergman: for he, to a great extent, was responsible for the literary respectability that cinema acquired in the late Fifties. On the subject of film's relationship to literature, Bergman himself has written, "Film has nothing to do with literature; the character and substance of the two art forms are usually in conflict"[1]— seemingly a rather ironical statement from a filmmaker of whom Jörn Donner has written, "No director has ever come to film with such a great reliance on literature, with such a pronounced affinity with his country's literary culture."[2]

Ingmar Bergman was born in 1918 in Uppsala, Sweden, the son of a Protestant minister. He studied literature and art at the University of Stockholm (where he was also active in amateur dramatics), and, very significantly, as we shall see later, wrote his university thesis on the Nineteenth century Swedish playwright August Strindberg. After completing his university studies, Bergman devoted his time to the writing of novels, short stories and plays; and he was also, for a short time, the director of a small repertoire theater. Then, in 1942, Bergman went to work for a large Swedish motion picture studio (Svensk Filmindustri), where he began his film career as a scriptwriter.

Bergman's importance in any serious study of film stems partly from the fact that he is one of the few true artists working in the commercial cinema today—having made over thirty films, most of which he has both written and directed himself. Even more importantly, he has had almost complete artistic control over his work, with little or no studio interference.

Bergman's films can be divided into roughly three periods (the first two of these three subdivisions were originally proposed by English critic Peter Cowie[3]). In his first nine films, starting with *Torment* (*Hets,* 1944—for which he wrote the script only) and ending with *To Joy* (*Till glädje,* 1950), one theme appears dominant: "Life is Hell on Earth," with the subsidiary theme, "Man's loneliness." In his middle period, Peter Cowie tells us, Bergman is apparently "preoccupied with the study of women and the psychology of their relations with men."[4] Also evident in some of these films of Bergman's middle period is the *motif* of the Scandinavian summer, with all its mystery and beauty. Bergman's later films, of his third period, are much too complex to be easily categorized. They include consummate but rather stiff and theatrical comedies, films with religious, philosophical and moral themes, and, lastly, rather incomprehensible personal statements. The film that we shall examine in this chapter, *Wild Strawberries* (*Smultronstället,* 1957), is somewhat of a maverick, not easily related to Bergman's other films, but like his *The Magician* (*Ansiktet,* 1958), it possesses a remarkable humanistic quality. Besides the fact that it is extremely well written, *Wild Strawberries* offers a rich and fascinating example of the literary possibilities of the narrative form in film; in fact, it has even been called a novel in film form.[5] Since both the content and the sequence of events of this film are crucial to the understanding of its complexities, what will follow is a very detailed synopsis— more detailed than any other to be included in this book.

Synopsis

Like Bresson's *Diary of a Country Priest, Wild Strawberries* is a first person *narratage* (voice-over) given to us by Isak Borg, a seventy-six-year-old retired professor of medicine; and which, Borg tells us, is, as nearly as he can make it, a true account of the events, dreams and thoughts which befell him on a certain day. Although he declines to give us the reason for his story, he does promise to come back to that subject later on in his narrative.

As in *Diary of a Country Priest,* the first shot shows the protagonist writing in a diary (the influence of Bresson on Bergman is unmistakably clear in this film). The story that the protagonist, Isak, writes in his diary begins on the morning that he is to go from his home in Stockholm to the University at Lund, where he is to receive an honorary degree for his long and devoted service to medicine.* Isak begins his narrative by telling us that, of his own free will, he has withdrawn almost completely from society, and therefore has found himself rather alone in his old age—all he asks from life at this point is to be left alone and allowed to devote himself to the "superficial" things which continue to interest him, such as keeping up with his profession, golf and a good detective story now and then. He even candidly

---

* I have based this synopsis primarily on the published screenplay (in English), and therefore there may be some minor discrepancies compared with the completed film, where a great deal of Isak's first-person narration has been omitted. Any major discrepancy between screenplay and film will be duly noted, however.

admits to being an old pedant and hard to get along with. After giving this brief and not particularly flattering picture of himself, Isak recalls a strange and very unpleasant dream that he had early that morning, and in which, among other frightening things that are meant to be symbolic, he sees himself as a corpse; at this point he awakens. (Isak confesses to us that this is not the first time he has had such a frightening dream; in fact, he has been haunted by them over the past few years. However, this is the first admission on Isak's part that beneath the outward appearance of self-satisfied stoicism that he projects, all may not be well.)

Now that he is awake, Isak knows immediately what he must do: he will drive by car to the ceremonies at Lund, instead of taking the plane as previously arranged. This sudden change in plans brings an immediate cry of consternation from his aging housekeeper (Miss Agda), but Isak, his mind made up, is not to be deterred. Marianne, his daughter-in-law (who has been staying with Isak because of marital difficulties with his son Evald, also a physician), asks if she can join him on the car trip to Lund, where she plans to rejoin her husband—a request which Isak appears only too happy to grant.

At the start of the journey, the coolness of the relationship between Isak and his daughter-in-law is clearly delineated. Isak reminds Marianne that he and his son are very much alike: they both have their principles; and it is for this reason that Isak requires repayment of a loan which enabled Evald to complete his medical studies, even though Isak knows that it is difficult for his son to repay him. "A bargain is a bargain," says Isak, to which his daughter-in-law bitterly replies that even his own son hates him, adding that he is also inconsiderate and an egotist. Marianne further chides Isak for taking no interest whatsoever in her and Evald's marital problems. Isak demurs and tells Marianne that he is really very fond of her; but, beyond that, he appears to pay no attention to her bitter castigations.

The journey continues in silence, until suddenly Isak has an impulse to stop at a nearby old country house where he spent many happy summers as a youth. Near this house Isak locates a wild strawberry patch, which used to be one of his childhood haunts. Here he is overcome with a strange feeling of solemnity—"as if this were a day of decision." Miraculously, the strange reality of this day begins to flow for Isak in dream-like images (part dreams and part memories). The first of these images to appear is Sara, Isak's cousin, whom he was to marry when he was twenty—she later married his brother Sigfrid—and whom we see picking wild strawberries for their Uncle Aron's birthday; Isak can see and hear her, but she cannot see or hear him. Shortly, Isak's brother Sigfrid finds Sara in the strawberry patch and wastes no time in making advances. Sara tries to ward him off by saying that she and Isak are secretly engaged, but Sigfrid is undaunted. Suddenly the gong rings announcing the family breakfast, a scene which Bergman depicts with great sensitivity and comic detail; and in which Sara confesses that she finds Sigfrid more exciting than Isak, although she realizes that Sigfrid does not possess Isak's fine qualities. Abruptly, Isak is awakened from his dream by a young woman, also named Sara (and played by the same actress who plays his cousin), who asks him if he will give a lift to her and her two boyfriends—Anders and Viktor (the three are on their way to Italy for a holiday). The new Sara is rather like the old—impetuous and flippant—and Isak takes an immediate liking to her, readily agreeing to the lift.

As Isak is driving along with his four companions—Marianne, Sara, Anders and Viktor—a small black car suddenly appears from around a curve, heading straight towards them; Isak immediately brakes to a stop, while the other car turns over in a ditch. The two occupants—while still in the midst of a violent quarrel—crawl out of their overturned vehicle and introduce themselves to Isak and his party: the driver is named Alman, an electrical engineer; the other occupant is his wife Berit, a former actress. With the couple's car completely inoperable, Isak offers the two a ride to the nearest gas station. Once inside the car, however, the couple continue their bickering: Alman ridicules his wife for her hysteria, and she, in turn, ridicules him for being a Catholic. Finally, Marianne, who is now driving, stops the car and asks the couple to please get out for the sake of the three young people riding with them; Alman and Berit obey like two scolded school children, leaving Isak and his party to continue their journey in peace.

After driving for quite some time, Isak and his companions stop at a gas station located in a part of Sweden where Isak first began his medical practice many years ago. Åkerman, the owner, immediately recognizes and greets Isak, reminding him of the high esteem in which he is held among the towns-people for his dedication and humanity as their local doctor. Isak and his party drive to a nearby country inn, where they enjoy a leisurely outdoor lunch. During the meal, Anders, who is studying for the ministry, and Viktor, who is a medical student, enter into an argument concerning the existence of God. Anders, as one would expect, champions a theological view, while Viktor remains a skeptic. Sara asks Isak to mediate in the argument, but he declines, reciting instead a few lines of verse which amount to "a pantheistic salute to life,"[6] by a Nineteenth century Swedish poet. After the luncheon, Isak and Marianne leave their three young companions for a short while and visit Isak's ninety-six-year-old mother who lives nearby. She lives alone (attended only by a nurse) and is a very disquieting person—the mother of ten children, she has outlived them all except for Isak and now spends her time trying to remember the birthdays of her numerous grand-children and great-grand-children, most of whom she has never seen.

When Isak and Marianne return to the inn, they learn from Sara that Anders and Viktor's metaphysical argument has now escalated into a fist fight; Marianne, however, calms down the two hotheads, and the journey commences once again.

While Marianne drives, Isak drifts off into sleep and experiences some rather humiliating dreams. Before recounting these dreams for us, Isak remarks that he does not intend to comment on their possible meaning. While not particularly enthusiastic about the psycho-analytical theory of dreams, he does admit, however, that "in these dreams there was something like a warning"; he also admits that during the last few years he has glided rather easily into memories and dreams that are highly personal, and he wonders if this is not a sign of increasing senility or perhaps "a harbinger of approaching death."

In this particular dream, Isak finds himself once again in the wild strawberry patch of his childhood; his cousin Sara (again as a young woman) is also there. She holds up a mirror so that Isak can see how old and ugly he is, and then says to him, "You are a worried old man who will die soon, but I have my whole life before me . . ." His reflection in the mirror and Sara's harsh words are painful for Isak; but Sara feels no compassion and belittles Isak for not knowing why it hurts him: "In spite of all your knowledge you don't really know anything," she cruelly says, and then runs into a nearby house where Isak's brother Sigfrid is waiting. Isak follows Sara and is met at the door by the man he picked up on the road earlier that day, Mr. Alman, who invites him inside to a large room that resembles a medical amphitheater. Here, before a small audience, Alman subjects Isak to an examination of his competence as a physician—which Isak fails. (One of the questions that Alman asks, but Isak cannot answer, is, "What is a doctor's first duty?" The answer: To ask forgiveness.) Not only does Isak fail the examination, but, Alman informs Isak, he is also "guilty of guilt"; Isak is also accused (by his deceased wife) of "some smaller but nonetheless serious offenses"—"indifference, selfishness, lack of consideration." After presenting Isak with the charges,

Alman leads him to a clearing in a forest, where he is made to witness a scene of many years before: his wife committing adultery with another man. In this same scene, Isak's wife tells her lover that she will go home and tell her husband what she has done, and he will say that he forgives her; but he is really a hypocrite, because he is too cold to feel anything about anybody. Isak, after witnessing this scene, calmly asks Alman what his penalty will be. Alman sternly replies that his punishment is the usual one: loneliness.

Suddenly, Isak wakes from his dream to find that the car has stopped alongside the road near a forest; his young companions are exercising their legs, and only Marianne remains in the car. Isak tells her about his dreams, saying that they seem to be telling him something he does not want to hear when awake—that he is spiritually dead, although still living. Marianne replies that he and Evald are very much alike, that her husband has told her he too feels dead inside. She then recounts for Isak an incident that happened a few months before, when she and Evald had gone out for a drive. At that time, Marianne tells Isak, she took the opportunity to tell her husband she was pregnant and was intent on having the child (there is an implication here that she had previously undergone at least one abortion). Evald was not encouraged by the news, and reminded Marianne that he himself was the product of a dismal marriage, chiding her for being so brazen as to want to bring a child into a world as absurd as the present. Evald then issued an ultimatum: his wife must choose between him or the child. Marianne, however, refused to give up the baby. (Her description of this encounter is shown in flashback.)

Isak and his party continue their journey, arriving at the city of Lund just before the ceremonies are due to begin. In a scene omitted from the completed film, Isak is placed in a special room (while the ceremonies are being arranged) in the company of two old men who are also to receive honorary degrees that day: the former Bishop Jakob Hovelius, who was an old schoolmate of Isak, and Carl-Adam Tiger, a former Professor of Roman Law. The ceremonies are somber and dull, but during them, Isak confesses to us, he began to see a remarkable causality in the chain of events of that day.

That night, as Isak prepares for bed, his three young companions come to sing him a serenade and say goodbye before they leave. Isak wishes them good luck on their journey and then returns to his bed. Before falling off to sleep, he speaks briefly with his son; Evald tells his father that Marianne will return to him (Evald), for he cannot live without her, even if it means that he must acquiesce to her desire to have the child. Isak raises the subject of the loan—with the purpose of telling his son that he is cancelling the obligation to pay it back—but Evald misunderstands and resentfully tells his father that he will get his money in due course. Marianne joins her husband in Isak's bedroom, and a *rapprochement* forms between her and her father-in-law. "I like you, Marianne," says Isak. "I like you, too, Father Isak," she replies. Evald and Marianne leave the room to go to a faculty ball, and the film ends as Isak drifts off into sleep and dreams a pleasant dream about his childhood.

Although on first viewing one is usually struck with the extreme beauty and gentleness of *Wild Strawberries,* it is far from being a simple film; in fact, it abounds in complexities—from style, to structure, to meaning. In terms of direct continuity (which comprises the external structure of the film), *Wild Strawberries* appears straight-forward enough: the events and dreams that Isak Borg experiences on a certain day. Beyond this, however, there appears to be little agreement among critics about what else does or does not occur. For instance, it is not altogether clear whether or not Isak undergoes any significant change of character during the film. In this regard, Birgitta Steene sees *Wild Strawberries* as a *search* by Isak for peace and self-knowledge, at the end of which he gains *insight* into himself and "can rest peacefully reconciled with his son and daughter-in-law."[7] Characterizing *Wild Strawberries* as a search, however, seems questionable: in order for there to be a search there must be determination, of which the only sign on Isak's part is after the first dream, when he inexplicably decides to drive to the ceremonies at Lund instead of taking the plane—hardly enough determination to be worthy of mention. There is little indication of insight also. It is true that Isak confesses to Marianne his interpretation of the dreams, but if this is to be construed as a significant gain of insight on Isak's part— significant in the sense that its discovery brings about a change of character within him—it would surely have to be the plot climax of the film; this it is not.

The only time that Isak appears to have any real awareness of what is happening to him is during the ceremonies at Lund, when he remarks that he "was beginning to see a re-markable causality in this chain of unexpected, entangled events."[8] However, this inkling of awareness is not elabo-rated further in the film; thus, the hope that Isak did, in fact, gain insight into himself has to be abandoned, even though, from a humanistic standpoint, we do so with great reluctance. It is indeed true, as Birgitta Steene states, that Isak rests peacefully at the film's end; but it is not at all apparent that this state of peacefulness is more than just temporary, since the cause of Isak's nightmares has not been removed.* It is also true that Isak is reconciled with his daughter-in-law at the end of the film, but the reconciliation with his son seems more illusory, as the misunderstanding

---

* From a Freudian point of view, the cause of Isak's anxiety, as expressed in many of his dreams, is most certainly the unresolved neurotic problems of his childhood. However, the identities of these conflicts are only vaguely hinted at in the film; and from a psycho-analytic view, no attempt is made by Isak either to uncover and/or resolve them. In fact, at one point in the screenplay, Isak remarks that he has never really subscribed to the psycho-analytic interpretation of dreams and has not the slightest intention of commenting on their possible meaning—although he does look upon them as some kind of warning. (We shall soon have occasion to examine other Freudian aspects of this film.)

over the status of the loan would indeed suggest.

Peter Cowie has written that in *Wild Strawberries* Isak Borg "is brought to the utmost anguish before he discerns any solution to his problems."[9] Cowie's observation about Isak's anguish is certainly justifiable, for many of the things that take place during the film are indeed painful for him to watch and remember; on the other hand, Cowie's assertion that Isak discerns a solution to his problems is not as plausible, for nowhere in the film does Isak mention to us that he has any problems of consequence (except possibly his frequent nightmares), and, least of all, does Isak give us the impression that he discerns any solutions (except when he says, at the end of the film, "Whenever I am restless or sad, I usually try to recall memories from my childhood to calm down"[10]).

I mentioned earlier in this chapter that this film bears certain similarities to Robert Bresson's *Diary of a Country Priest*. One is their both being spiritual dramas, or, in other words, about the spiritual lives of their protagonists. In this regard, Eugene Archer alleges that in the examination scene, Isak "is able to accept his sentence—solitude, with understanding of its justice and its meaning," and therefore "he is finally ready for his Christian rebirth."[11] And in the same vein, Birgitta Steene sees *Wild Strawberries* as "a confessional drama in the tradition of Strindberg's "To Damascus." Like the Stranger in Strindberg's play, Isak Borg goes through the stages of a Christian confession: acknowledgement of guilt, penance, and absolution. . . . Isak's search [like the Stranger's] explores the possibilities of love and fellowship, ending in a mellow acceptance of life."[12] These spiritual interpretations of *Wild Strawberries* by Eugene Archer and Birgitta Steene are certainly plausible; unfortunately, though, there is little evidence in either the film or the screenplay to confirm or deny them.

Jörn Donner gives an analysis of *Wild Strawberries* that is, I believe, the most credible; he writes that Isak "has lived

his life in peace of mind and cynicism, but that he, toward
the end, can win peace of mind and still relinquish cynicism."[13] Indeed, as Donner indicates, Isak gives every impression of having achieved peace of mind at the film's
beginning, stating bluntly, "All I ask of life is to be left alone
and to have the opportunity to devote myself to the few
things which continue to interest me . . ."[14] Isak also admits
that he has found himself rather alone in his old age, but
of his own volition and with no regrets. However, whether
Isak does, in fact, relinquish his cynicism in the end seems
questionable: Isak may appear to be a more agreeable person
at the end of the film than at the beginning, but nothing that
occurs during his day-long journey actually alters his basic
outlook on life. Besides, from the point of view of dramaturgy, what would really be the point of there being such a
change anyway? At the age of seventy-six, what effect on his
own life and the lives of others could such a change have?
His wife is dead; and even when he offers, somewhat belatedly, to intercede on Marianne's behalf in her marriage
to his son, Evald, he is told by his daughter-in-law that such
intervention would be futile: "We [Marianne and Evald]
are too old . . . It has gone too far."[15] And as for Isak's
gesture to cancel the repayment of the loan to his son, can
it really have much effect on the rather acrimonious relationship that has existed between them for so many years?

According to the laws of dramatic construction, because
Isak does not attempt to resolve any conflicts that might
involve him (as he admits to having none), he, therefore,
cannot logically be the focal point of a plot structure. That
is not to say, however, that *Wild Strawberries* is entirely
plotless; there is a minor one involving Evald, in whom we
can quite clearly recognize a definite inner conflict: the
warmth and hopefulness of his wife Marianne *versus* the
cold and cynical influence of his father, Isak. What is more,
we see that this conflict has reached a crisis point; for, as
Marianne tells Isak after their visit to his mother, she fears

that "Evald is on the verge of becoming just as lonely and cold—and dead [as Isak and his mother]."[16] Thus, we have the urgency of saving Evald; Isak and his mother, unfortunately, are too far advanced—there is nothing that can be done to save them—but perhaps there is enough time left to save Evald from the same dreadful fate.*

Simply because Isak undergoes no great fundamental change in his character, it does not mean that nothing significant happens to him during the film. In fact, Isak is able, for the first time in his life (both waking and dream), to give vent to feelings and emotions that have been heretofore internalized and repressed. This is only vaguely apparent, however, in the screenplay—e.g. after Marianne tells him of Evald's coldness, Isak tells us, "I suddenly felt shaken in a way which I had never experienced before"[17]—but it is quite apparent in the performance of Victor Sjöström (who plays Isak) and the way in which Bergman has directed the film. The final result of this vague sort of catharsis that Isak appears to undergo can be seen at the end of the film in Isak's increased *rapprochement* with his daughter-in-law and his attempt at eliminating the stiff formality in his relationship with his housekeeper.

The Dreams in Wild Strawberries

Much of the confusion that *Wild Strawberries* has caused critics is due, I believe, to the ambiguous nature of its dream sequences, which make up a good part of the film. No one appears more confused by them than Isak himself, for he confides to us (in the screenplay) that during the last few years he has glided "rather easily into a twilight world of

---

* The situations of Isak and his mother are hopeless from Marianne's point of view. Also, the reader may have noted that Marianne's attitude toward her husband and her marriage is sometimes contradictory. In one instance she notes the urgency of saving both, and then, shortly afterward, she admits to the hopelessness of the situation.

memories and dreams which are highly personal. I've often wondered if this is a sign of increasing senility. Sometimes I've also asked myself if it is a harbinger of approaching death."[18] These questions are never really answered in the film or the screenplay; we are therefore left to speculate whether, at an advanced age, Isak—or anyone else for that matter—might not have frequent and highly personal dreams no matter how he had lived his life. This should not be taken to mean, however, that the individual dreams in *Wild Strawberries* have no real meaning; a statement such as that would be absurd because even Isak himself recognises that they have significance—although he may not be sure exactly what that significance is.

From a Freudian point of view, Isak's dreams are not at all difficult to interpret, since they consist primarily of un-disguised wish-fulfillments (e.g. the desire to relive the more happy moments of his childhood) and ordinary memories (e.g. recollections of his childhood and his wife's infidelity), some of which are painful for him.* And even in those dreams where there is an appreciable difference between *manifest* content (i.e. the details, or text, of a dream as re-tained in the memory of the dreamer) and *latent* content (i.e. the dream's *actual* meaning), the latent content is usu-ally unmistakably clear, especially to Isak: his repressed feel-ings of guilt and spiritual sterility (e.g. "I'm dead, although I live"[19]). As we shall see shortly, the importance of the dreams in *Wild Strawberries* lies not so much in any insights into Isak that they may provide—and they do provide a num-ber of them—but in the fact that they are the major source of the film's internal logic, or, in other words, they provide its structural principle.†

---

* I have yet to offer an interpretation of the first dream of the film, in which Isak sees himself as a corpse. Although Bergman employs a great deal of symbolism in this particular dream, its meaning is fairly well agreed upon: it is a repressed fear, on the part of Isak, of impending death.

† In regard to the influence of Freud on the depiction of the dreams and their contents in Bergman's film, it is interesting to note that in his *The*

Rather surprisingly, the internal logic—dream logic, that is—of *Wild Strawberries* comes to Bergman not so much from Freud (whose name is almost synonymous with dream theory) but from August Strindberg, who, as we have already mentioned, was the subject of Bergman's university thesis. In the introduction to his *A Dream Play* (from which Bergman has drawn at least some of the symbolism for his film), Strindberg very eloquently expressed what, unmistakably, must have served as the model for *Wild Strawberries*'s inner structure.

The famed Swedish playwright begins by saying that in his play he "has sought to reproduce the disconnected but apparently logical form of a dream," where "on a slight groundwork of reality, imagination spins and weaves new patterns made up of memories, experiences, unfettered fancies, absurdities and improvisations." Strindberg then says that although the characters in his play "are split, double and multiply . . . evaporate, crystallise, scatter and converge, . . . a single consciousness holds sway over them all—that of the dreamer. For him there are no secrets, no incongruities, no scruples and no law. He neither condemns nor acquits, but only relates, and since on the whole, there is more pain than pleasure in the dream, a tone of melancholy, and of compassion for all living things, runs through the swaying narrative."[20]

We can find reference to this same dream logic, but expressed a little differently, in the screenplay for *Wild Straw-*

Interpretation of Dreams—ed. and trans. by James Strachey, Standard ed. (New York, Basic Books, Inc., 1953), pp. 130-131—Freud presents two rather interesting children's dreams as examples of simple wish-fulfillments: the first, a dream by his daughter Anna (then nineteen months old) in which she dreamt of eating some wild strawberries; the second, a dream about eating some cherries, which was dreamt by his nephew (then twenty-two months old), who earlier that day had been entrusted with the duty of presenting his uncle (Sigmund Freud himself) with a basket of cherries on his (Freud's) birthday. The reader may note the similarity between these two dreams—especially the second one—and Isak's dream of his cousin Sara gathering a basket of wild strawberries to present to their Uncle Aron on his birthday.

berries itself, where (in the omitted scene) the Bishop Jakob Hovelius says to Isak, "As Schopenhauer says somewhere, 'Dreams are a kind of lunacy and lunacy a kind of dream.' But life is also supposed to be a kind of dream isn't it?"[21] And perhaps Schopenhauer's statement should be compared with one by Freud: "A dream, then, is a psychosis, with all the absurdities, delusions and illusions of a psychosis."[22]

There is one particular element in both the film and the screenplay of *Wild Strawberries* that tends to obscure the real logic of this work—its dream logic—and that element is the trial atmosphere that pervades much of the film. Throughout the screenplay, especially, there are very subtle implications that Isak will be made to face some sort of judgement. The first inkling of this comes just before the second dream sequence, when Isak tells us that he was overcome with "a strange feeling of solemnity, as if this were a day of decision."[23] Also, most of the characters in the film pass judgements—good and bad—on Isak. Finally, this apparent trial atmosphere crystallizes into an actual arraignment—in the examination dream sequence, where Isak is found "guilty of guilt" and sentenced to loneliness (rather belatedly considering the fact that Isak had already been so condemned many years before). However, the risk that Bergman runs in employing this device is that we, the audience, may be tempted to weigh the evidence—which is equally convincing on both sides—and render a verdict for or against Isak. To return again to Strindberg's exposition of dream logic, the dreamer "neither condemns nor acquits, but only relates . . . [while] a tone of melancholy, and of compassion for all living things, runs through the swaying narrative." That is exactly what Bergman's *mise-en-scène* would suggest to us—that we are not to pass judgement on Isak Borg, but feel compassion for him instead.* Because of its rather unique internal logic—which

---

* Very close in sympathy to this Strindbergian dream logic are the Proustian overtones that critic Eugene Archer detects in this film; he observes that the wild strawberries in Bergman's film

overshadows the entire production—both the theme and premise of *Wild Strawberries,* very strong in their own right, are sometimes overlooked.

Theme and premise

The major theme of *Wild Strawberries* is essentially a statement concerning man's loneliness—and we are first introduced to it on the first page of the screenplay, where Isak tells us that he has been rather alone in his old age. We find this same theme developed further when Isak and Marianne visit his mother, who is also very much alone. In the dream sequence in which Isak fails his examination and is made to witness again his wife's infidelity, we have the thematic climax of the film: Isak's punishment is to be loneliness. The premise of *Wild Strawberries* is a very familiar one with Bergman—that despite all his knowledge man really knows very little, and especially about himself—an idea fully articulated in the dream in which Sara tells Isak, "In spite of all your knowledge you don't really know anything,"[25] and later exemplified in the same dream, when Isak cannot read on a blackboard the first duty of a physician: *"to ask forgiveness."*[26] These are by no means the only themes and premises in *Wild Strawberries:* there is the theme expressed by the symbiotic misery of the bickering couple, Alman and Berit, which appears so frequently in Bergman's films: Hell together is better than Hell alone. There is also the premise that is amply demonstrated by the arguments of Viktor and Anders, and later succinctly stated (in the omitted scene) by Isak's long-time friend Bishop Jakob Hovelius just before the

---

are the equivalent of Marcel Proust's famed *petite madeleine* which the narrator dips into a cup of tea to commence his "A la Recherche du temps perdu."

The essence of Proust's image, and Bergman's, is the conception that an event assumes its meaning, not from the action itself, but from the way it is regarded at different moments in time, and that life is composed of a series of such isolated moments, given meaning by their temporal relationship to the memories of the man who experiences them.[24]

ceremonies at Lund: All arguments over metaphysical questions come to nothing.

Orchestration

Besides being a finely-wrought work, *Wild Strawberries* is also finely textured—with its texture being derived primarily from Bergman's skilful orchestration of emotions, characters and style. In this one film, Bergman evokes such contrasting emotions as pathos and shock; presents characters that are comic, warm, pitiful and cold; and utilizes such contrasting styles as lyricism and expressionism. It is for all these reasons that *Wild Strawberries* stands even today as Bergman's one true film masterpiece. Stanley Kauffmann, however, finds Bergman's film dissatisfying because, as he says, "Without growth, the picture does not fulfil a fundamental requirement of drama: the protagonist is unchanged at the end."[27] Yet, the very thing that Kauffmann finds wrong with *Wild Strawberries* is the very thing that gives this film its artistic distinction—for by loosening the fetters of classical dramaturgy, Bergman has brought the cinema to a level of greater artistic maturity, in the tradition, as we have already seen, of Robert Bresson's *Diary of a Country Priest* and neo-realism.* Before we complete this brief exposition of Ingmar Bergman's genius, we should, perhaps, examine some of his ideas on filmmaking, since they shed valuable light on the creative aspects of this artistic process, especially the first stage—the idea or writing stage.

Bergman on Filmmaking

The best source material for Bergman's approach to filmmaking is his introduction to the English translation of four of his screenplays—one of which is *Wild Strawberries.*[28] Here

---

* In a later chapter we shall see how this particular aspect of *Wild Strawberries* has had a profound effect on Federico Fellini.

Bergman tells us that, for him, a film begins as "something very vague—a chance remark or a bit of conversation, a hazy but agreeable event unrelated to any particular situation. It can be a few bars of music, a shaft of light across the street."[29] From these first stirrings emerge "vibrations and rhythms which are very special and unique to each film"[30]— and it is from these elements that Bergman will pattern the picture sequences of his film. If these embryonic substances prove viable enough, a film will emerge.

The next stage, Bergman tells us, is exceedingly difficult, consisting of the "transformation of rhythms, moods, atmosphere, tensions, sequences, tones and scents into words and sentences, into an understandable screenplay"[31]—something that Bergman admits is almost an impossible task, in which only the dialogue can be satisfactorily rendered. (When writing dialogue, he prefers not to include directions on how it should be delivered—its rhythm and tempo and what takes place between the lines—otherwise a screenplay so detailed, Bergman feels, would be completely unreadable; also, he tries to write his instructions of location, characterization and atmosphere in the clearest and most understandable terms possible, something which, even he admits, he is not always successful in doing.) In regard to this writing stage, Bergman finds that the screenplay is an inadequate medium for clearly indicating the visual qualities of his films, especially the way in which they are to be edited and the relationship between shots; in short, it is impossible for Bergman to indicate in the screenplay how a film will breathe and pulsate. Bergman adds that frequently during the shooting of a film he becomes so bogged down in the trivial details of production that he loses sight of his original conception and the continuity of the film; it is for this reason that he wishes there were some kind of system of notation by which he could put on paper "all the shades and tones of . . . [his] vision, to record distinctly the inner structure of a film."[32] Thus, the script—in its present state of evolution—is for Bergman only "a very imperfect technical basis for a film";[33] however, Bergman finds its writing an extremely useful, albeit difficult, exercise, for it compels him to first prove logically on paper the validity of his film ideas.

8

Stream of Consciousness
in the Novel and Film

Stream of consciousness is a technique used to depict mental states that is common to film and the novel—although it originated with and has been used more frequently in the latter. The different ways in which this technique has been employed in these two separate media can provide us with some very important insights into the differences between novel and film, and therefore will be the subject of this chapter.*

The term "stream of consciousness" comes to us not from literature but psychology; it was coined at the turn of the century by the American psychologist William James to describe metaphorically the nature of conscious mental ac-

---

* In the preparation of this chapter, I found Robert Humphrey's book *Stream of Consciousness in the Modern Novel* (Berkeley and Los Angeles, University of California Press, 1954) to be an invaluable aid.

tivity. According to James, "Consciousness . . . does not appear to itself chopped up in bits. Such words as 'chain' or 'train' do not describe it fitly as it presents itself in the first instance. It is nothing jointed; it flows. A 'river' or a 'stream' are the metaphors by which it is most naturally described."[1] Apt as William James's metaphor may be, it can provide us with only a vague understanding of consciousness, so we shall now examine the processes and components that are collectively referred to as "consciousness" in order to gain a clearer understanding of this concept.

What is consciousness?

Consciousness can be said to be all the mental processes that occur when we are awake; dreams, on the other hand, as our consciousness when we are asleep, of which we are directly aware or capable of being directly aware. Some of these processes are memory, imagination or fantasy, sensory perception—including seeing and hearing—and verbal, mathematical and spatial reasoning. However, since most cultures are verbally oriented, that which is most commonly associated with consciousness is verbal thought; thus, the following discussion will emphasize the verbal side of consciousness —although this should not be taken to mean that there is any personal bias on the part of the author toward one form or another.

Not only are there different processes that comprise consciousness, there are also different levels of these processes, usually referred to as "levels of consciousness." The most commonly used standard for designating these has its basis in verbal syntax and logic—with formal, grammatically-correct language held as the highest level of consciousness, and syntactically-garbled thought, writing and speech as the lowest. In other words, at one end of the spectrum (the highest level), we have unity, clarity and coherence, and at the other end (the lowest level), we have the incomprehensible and incoherent. (Since in this chapter we are going to be primarily concerned with thought, we shall exclude both spoken and written communication from our discussion, and consider the level of consciousness just below speech or writing [pre-speech] as the highest level of consciousness.) Somewhere in-between these two poles are processes that violate the usual rules of syntax, logic and coherence—but for a purpose related to rhetoric, symbolism and imagery.*

Thus, the levels of consciousness (as regards verbal thought) can be thought of as similar to the stages in the writing of an essay or story: the most rudimentary stage consists of only a few, hastily scribbled notes or impressions, which are continually revised and refined through several drafts into a version, characterized by its clarity, logic and coherence.

The flow of consciousness

Now that we have seen that conscious states may differ qualitatively, let us return to William James's metaphor of the "stream" and see just how conscious thought material "flows" through the mind. James made a very important observation, that within this "stream" of consciousness there are "sudden *contrasts in quality*"[2]: thus, memory may be juxtaposed with fantasy, the articulate juxtaposed with the inarticulate, and sensation juxtaposed with reflection.† Here two terms are very important: the *will* and *free association*.

---

* It certainly could be argued that these imagist processes—which really belong to the realm of art—should be rated at a higher level of consciousness than rational, syntactical thought. However, since studies have shown that rudimentary, imagist thought-processes can be observed in children before they have mastered logical thinking, I have not rated these processes as being of the highest level of consciousness for the purpose of this discussion (see David Elkind's article "Giant in the Nursery—Jean Piaget" in The New York *Times* Magazine, May 26, 1968).

† Here James uses the word "quality" to refer not only to the different levels of consciousness but also to their different processes, such as memory, sensory perception and imagination.

The former is probably the more familiar since it refers to a psychological component controlling memory, imagination and reflection. The term "free association" may be less familiar because it refers to a mental process that we are seldom aware of occurring (although it is probably the most frequent type of mental activity)—in brief, the *flow* of the stream of consciousness when the will is absent from the mind (sometime called *involuntary* thought).* In this mental state, thoughts pass rapidly through the mind: memory, fantasy, physical sensation, etc., are juxtaposed in an apparently random order—*apparently* random because we are not usually aware of the means or manner or logic by which these thoughts are associated with each other; but related they are, however minutely.† The stream of consciousness can thus be thought of as being the function of two important variables: *quality* and *flow*—two factors of which the successful depiction has long been a major stumbling block in the rendering of mental activity in both literature and film.

The Stream of Consciousness Novel

With the emergence of the psychological novel in the Nineteenth century, the mental activity of literary characters

---

* Freud considered this state of mind as analogous to that which exists just prior to sleep: " 'involuntary ideas' emerge owing to the relaxation of certain deliberate (and no doubt also critical) activity which we allow to influence the course of our ideas while we are awake. . . . As the involuntary ideas emerge they change into visual and acoustic images. . . ."[3] He induced in his patients undergoing psycho-analysis a state quite similar to that of involuntary thought to help them analyze their own dreams; however, in order for the patient to arrive at this mental state within himself, it was necessary for him first to exert a certain amount of will-power. The patient in achieving this state had to purposely abandon all deliberate and critical thinking and employ "the psychical energy thus saved (or a portion of it) in attentively following the involuntary thoughts which now emerge, and which . . . retain the character of ideas."[4]

† An important influence on this associative process is the "subconscious," another observation made by Freud; we shall discuss the ramifications of this observation in detail in Chapter Ten.

took on a new importance, but only in so far as it affected the novel's plot and revealed character motivation. Thoughts such as these—which reveal motivation and purposeful behavior—usually involve the upper levels of consciousness, and in the psychological novel were extracted from the stream of consciousness, excluding those thoughts that were more incoherent and less rational. It was only with the emergence of writers such as Dorothy Richardson, Virginia Woolf, James Joyce and William Faulkner in the first quarter of this century that there appeared what might be truly termed stream of consciousness fiction; these writers were not concerned with character thought as it affected plot, or even motivation, but with thought *per se:* their subject matter was consciousness, and therefore all levels of consciousness were depicted, not just the most rational and coherent.

Stream of Consciousness Techniques in the Novel

There are three major techniques commonly employed in fiction for depicting the stream of consciousness of a character: *direct interior monologue, indirect interior monologue* and *omniscient description.* The first technique presents the direct thoughts of a character—at the various levels of consciousness—to the reader with little or no intervention by the author (it is somewhat analogous to a direct quotation) ; this is generally the preferred method for depicting the lowest, most incoherent levels of consciousness and is usually written in the first person. The following is an excerpt from Molly Bloom's famous direct interior monologue at the end of James Joyce's *Ulysses;* note its partial incoherence (and the absence of punctuation) :

> . . . I suppose she was pious because no man would look at her twice I hope Ill never be like her a wonder she didnt want to cover our faces but she was a welleducated woman certainly and her gabby talk about Mr Riordan here and Mr Riordan there I suppose he was glad to get shut of her and her dog

smelling my fur and always edging to get up under my petti-
coats especially then still I like that in him polite to old women
like that and waiters and beggars too . . .[5]

In the second technique, indirect interior monologue, an
omniscient author also presents thought material as if it
comes directly from the consciousness of one of his characters
(somewhat like an indirect quotation), but along with occasional commentary and description that he may feel is necessary to guide the reader, and which is usually written in the
third person. Robert Humphrey gives the following excerpt
as an example of indirect interior monologue from Virginia
Woolf's novel "Mrs. Dalloway" (note that although the third
person is employed, the idioms are those of the character) :

> Mrs. Dalloway said she would buy the flowers herself.
> For Lucy had her work cut out for her. The doors would be
> taken off their hinges; Rumpelmayer's men were coming. And
> then, thought Clarissa Dalloway, what a morning—fresh as if
> issued to children on a beach.
> What a lark! What a plunge! For so it has always seemed to
> her, when, with a little squeak of the hinges, which she could
> hear now, she had burst open the French windows and plunged
> at Bourton into the open air. How fresh, how calm, stiller
> than this of course, the air was in the early morning; like the
> flap of a wave; the kiss of a wave, chill and sharp and yet (for
> a girl of eighteen as she then was) solemn, feeling as she did,
> standing there at the open window, that something awful was
> about to happen . . .[6]

In the last method for depicting stream of consciousness,
omniscient description, an omniscient author *describes* the
thoughts of the character, ignoring their idiomatic qualities
and concentrating, instead, on their substantive content.
Humphrey chose the following excerpt to illustrate this technique, from the second volume of Dorothy Richardson's
Pilgrimage:

> The little shock sent her mind feeling out along the road
> they had just left. She considered its unbroken length, its

shops, its treelessness. The wide thoroughfare, up which they now began to rumble, repeated it on a large scale. The pavements were wide causeways reached from the roadway by stone steps, three deep. The people passing along them were all alike. They were . . . She could find no word for the strange impression they made. It coloured the whole of the district through which they had come. It was part of the new world to which she was pledged to go on September 18th. It was her world already, and she had no words for it.[7]

It is important to understand that the above techniques go from little or no intervention by the author (direct interior monologue) to substantial intervention (omniscient description). We shall be primarily concerned with this important distinction when we next examine how these techniques have been employed in film.

Stream of Consciousness Techniques in Film

The techniques used for depicting stream of consciousness in film are essentially the same as those employed in the novel: direct interior monologue, indirect interior monologue and omniscient description—of which the first and last are most easily recognized by filmgoers. Direct interior monologue usually appears in the form of a voice-over that belongs to the main character (as in *Diary of a Country Priest*), and which tells what he or she is thinking or feeling; the third technique generally employs an omniscient narrator for the purpose of providing a voice-over that describes a particular character's thoughts or feeling—but usually not his own, if the narrator is also a character in the film (see the discussion on *narratage* in Chapter Six).

It is the second technique, indirect interior monologue, which is the hardest to discern in film, and for a very good reason: it is never actually spoken. We have already noted that rational, coherent verbal thought is not the only mental activity that takes place during consciousness: there is also sensory perception, and especially visual perception, which is also part of consciousness. Therefore, what a character (in both literature and film) may see is just as important in rendering a true stream of consciousness as what he may think or *feel*. Sometimes, in trying to present what a character sees (with a subjective camera*), a film director will intersperse this visual material—from the point of view of the character—with other shots that help to orient the audience, and which serve the same purpose as the occasional written commentary and description that a novelist may feel are necessary to guide his readers in a stream of consciousness passage. For example, a character sitting in an automobile sees a woman standing near his car; in such a case there may be a shot—with the camera located inside the car (shooting through the windshield)—of the woman the character is looking at, exactly as he sees her. However, the director may find it advisable for the audience to know just where this automobile is located, especially in relation to the woman; for that purpose he may call for an extreme long shot of the man sitting in the car, taken from outside the automobile—from the vantage point of an omniscient narrator, who is, in this case, the director and the camera. Thus, in the aforementioned example, the film director intrudes on the consciousness of the character (exemplified by the subjective shot from inside the car) with information that he feels is necessary to guide the viewer (conveyed through the long shot).

The three techniques described above only denote the vehicles for depicting the stream of consciousness (e.g. the character himself or an omniscient narrator or camera) and tell us nothing about the *flow* or *quality* of consciousness and how they are depicted in both the novel and film. For the remainder of this chapter, therefore, we shall concern ourselves with these two important aspects in the rendering of stream of consciousness in both media.

---

* A *subjective camera* is a shot taken from the point of view of one of the characters in a film, and usually at the same eye-level.

The Flow of Consciousness in the Novel and Film

In literature the most common device for indicating changes in the direction and flow of consciousness is punctuation, with dashes and ellipses being the marks most conventionally employed, although some authors have preferred to use other marks extensively: e.g. Faulkner, italics; Virginia Woolf, parentheses; and James Joyce, no punctuation at all. Another device commonly employed is verb tenses; these are sometimes the sole device for depicting changes occurring back and forth between thoughts representing the present, the past (memory), imagination and fantasy.

In film, the major device (visual) for indicating these changes—which are usually abrupt—is the direct cut; the direct juxtaposition of shots in this way can reproduce with great facility the actual juxtaposition of thoughts and sensations as they appear in the stream of consciousness. Since film has no tenses, the distortion of the photographed image is sometimes employed for the purpose of conveying a feeling of unreality—suggestive, perhaps, of memory, dreams or fantasy.

The Quality of Consciousness As Rendered in the Novel and Film

The qualitative aspects of the stream of consciousness, i.e. the varying levels of consciousness, have been depicted in literature through a number of different devices. The most prominent has been *syntax*, with the more garbled and incomprehensible the syntax of the thought material being depicted, the lower the level of consciousness being represented; on the other hand, the more coherent the syntax, the higher the level depicted. Somewhere between these two extremes is thought material that is primarily characterized

in literature by rhetoric, symbolism and verbal imagery—
e.g. metaphor and simile.

In film, the lowest and highest levels are the easiest to
express in purely visual terms;* the juxtaposition of shots
can be readily arranged to follow the corresponding verbal
syntax, which usually distinguishes these two opposite poles.

It is the levels of consciousness between the highest and
the lowest, however, that are the most difficult to portray
visually in film, i.e. the levels that exclusively employ imagist
constructions.

In an earlier chapter we noted that the metaphor, one of
the most common of all literary images, is apparently not
capable of being directly translated into film. Eisenstein was
one of the first filmmakers to make this discovery; he noted
that the development of the Soviet film, along with his own
theories of *montage,* went through a *"stage of excess in the
realm of the trope and primitive metaphor."*[8] The following
is an example provided by him of just such a naive attempt
at film metaphor, or trope (i.e. a figure of speech which uses
a word or phrase in a sense other than that which is usual) ;
it is contained in a description of a *montage* series from his
motion picture *October (Oktyabr,* 1927—also known by the
title *Ten Days That Shook the World)* :

> . . . we cut shots of harps and balalaikas into a scene of Men-
> sheviks addressing the Second Congress of Soviets. And these
> harps were shown not as harps, but as an imagist symbol of the
> mellifluent speech of Menshevik opportunism at the Congress.
> The balalaikas were not shown as balalaikas, but as the image
> of the tiresome strumming of these empty speeches in the face
> of the gathering storm of historical events. And placing side
> by side the Menshevik and the harp, the Menshevik and the
> balalaika, we were *extending the frame of parallel montage
> into a new quality, into a new realm:* from the sphere of *action*
> into the sphere of *significance.*[9]

---

* Of course, many film-makers have chosen to render consciousness and/or
the stream of consciousness in primarily verbal terms, i.e. through the
use of a voice-over.

Eisenstein provided another similar example from an even earlier film of his, *Strike* (*Stachka,* 1924) :

> The mass shooting of the demonstrators in the finale, interwoven with bloody scenes at the municipal slaughterhouse, merged . . . in a film-metaphor of "a human slaughterhouse . . .[10]

What then did Eisenstein propose as film's answer to the literary image—and thus the key to the visual rendering of imagist thought processes within the stream of consciousness? One possible solution that he proposed was *the visual image,* and more specifically, *the composition* or *framing of the shot.* In an earlier chapter we noted that one of the reasons for the artistic failure of Visconti's film adaptation of Camus's novel *The Stranger* was the naturalism of the photography *versus* the essence of the book; Eisenstein pointed to a similar problem in the film *Earth* (*Zemlya,* 1930), by another Russian filmmaker, Alexandr Dovzhenko—which he attributed to "a lack of awareness that for *imagist* and *extra-life-like* (or *surrealist*) 'manipulation' of film-shots there must be *an abstraction of the life-like representation.*"[11] The following is Eisenstein's analysis of how composition could have been advantageously employed in Dovzhenko's film:

> Such an abstraction of the life-like may in certain instances be given by the *close-up.*
> A healthy, handsome woman's body may, actually, be heightened to *an image of a life-affirming beginning,* which is what Dovzhenko had to have, to clash with his montage of the funeral in *Earth.*
> A skilfully leading montage creation with close-ups, taken in the "Rubens manner," isolated from naturalism and abstracted in the necessary direction, could well have been lifted to such a "sensually palpable" image.
> But the whole structure of *Earth* was doomed to failure, because in place of such montage material the director cut into the funeral *long shots* of the peasant hut, and the naked woman flinging herself about there. And the spectator could

not possibly separate out of this concrete, life-like woman that generalized sensation of blazing fertility, of sensual life-affirmation, which the director wished to convey of all nature, as a pantheistic contrast to the theme of death and the funeral! This was prevented by the ovens, pots, towels, benches, table-cloths—all those details of everyday life, from which the woman's body could easily have been freed by *the framing of the shot*,—so that *representational* naturalism would not interfere with the embodiment of the *conveyed metaphorical* task.[12]

We shall have more to say about composition, visual images and their application to the rendering of stream of consciousness in film in a later chapter.

Some New Approaches to Stream of Consciousness in Film

Eisenstein was not only concerned about the use of metaphor in film—and its possible application to the rendering of consciousness—but also the *whole* question of dealing with the stream of consciousness phenomenon in cinema. Fully knowledgeable of its application in the novel, Eisenstein believed that this psychological phenomenon could find its fullest artistic expression in film only.* In fact, he even went so far as to state that the laws of *montage*, as he had previously formulated and employed them in film, were actually only "a reconstruction of the laws of the thought process" as exemplified by "inner monologue," the term that he frequently used for "stream of consciousness."[13]

Not only did Eisenstein believe that the laws of inner monologue (or "inner speech," as he sometimes called it) determined those of film *montage*, he also believed that they provided the laws for all other art forms as well: "The laws of construction of inner speech turn out to be precisely those *laws which lie at the foundation of the whole variety of laws governing the construction of the form and composition of*

---

* Compare this with the footnote earlier in this chapter where Freud is quoted as having said: "As the involuntary ideas emerge they change into *visual* and *acoustic* images. . . ." [Italics are my own.]

art-works."[14] Eisenstein was aware, however, that the implication of such a bold assertion might be "that art is nothing
else but an artificial retrogression in the field of psychology
towards the forms of earlier thought-processes, i.e. the phenomenon identical with any given form of drug, alcohol, sha-
manism, religion, etc.!"[15] This, he believed, was not so; for
him a work of art was the result of a dialectical process:

> The affectiveness of a work of art is built upon the fact that
> there takes place in it a dual process: an impetuous progressive
> rise along the lines of the highest explicit steps of conscious-
> ness and a simultaneous penetration by means of the structure
> of the form into the layers of profoundest sensual thinking.
> The polar separation of these two lines of flow creates that
> remarkable tension of unity of form and content characteristic
> of true art-works.[16]

The failure of a work of art, according to Eisenstein, was
due to a lack of harmony of this dual process; or, as he
explained,

> By allowing one or the other element to predominate the
> art-work remains unfulfilled. A drive towards the thematic-
> logical side renders the work dry, logical, didactic. But over-
> stress on the side of the sensual forms of thinking with insuffi-
> cient account taken of the thematic-logical tendency—this is
> equally fatal for the work: the work becomes condemned to
> sensual chaos, elementalness, raving.[17]

Thus, for Eisenstein, a successful work of art was the result
of a balance between the thought-processes that are to be
found on first the lowest, and then the highest levels of consciousness.

Eisenstein was not simply interested in stream of consciousness as a theoretician; he actually intended to employ the
technique in one of his many film projects—an adaptation of
Theodore Dreiser's novel *An American Tragedy*, which he
planned to film in the United States. Dreiser's novel con-
cerns the supposed guilt or innocence of a young man named

Claude Laydu as the lonely curé of Bresson's film, Diary of a Country Priest. *Still courtesy of Audio Brandon Films.*

Isak Borg (Victor Sjöstrom) in the wild strawberry patch of his youth in the film Wild Strawberries. *Courtesy: Janus Films.*

Jean Paul Belmondo as Michel Poiccard, a "punk" with style. With him is Jean Seberg as Patricia, his American girl friend in Jean-Luc Godard's Breathless. *Contemporary Films/McGraw-Hill.*

Clyde, accused of murdering his girl-friend during a boat "accident" (something that Clyde had originally planned to do, but did not have the nerve to carry out). Eisenstein realized that the key sequence for the entire film would have to be the one that contained this alleged boat accident, and that he would need to depict this sequence with "an extraordinary differentiated sharpness of exposition of what was taking place within Clyde before that moment of the boat's 'accident' . . ."[18] However, Eisenstein found the author's literary approach to the problem, a rather "primitive" rhetoric, of little help; the following excerpt from Dreiser's novel illustrates this inadequacy:

> You might save her. But again you might not! For see how she strikes about. She is stunned. She herself is unable to save herself and by her erratic terror, if you draw near her now, may bring about your own death also. But you desire to live! And her living will make your life worth while from now on. Rest but a moment—a fraction of a minute! Wait—wait—ignore the pity of that appeal. And then—then—But there! Behold. It is over. She is sinking now. You will never, never see her alive any more—ever.[19]

The conventional methods employed in cinema at the time (*ca.* 1930) for such an exposition of a character's consciousness were also deemed inappropriate by Eisenstein. He noted:

> The whole arsenal of knitted brows, rolling eyes, hard breathing, contorted postures, stony faces, or close-ups of convulsively working hands, was inadequate for the expression of those subtleties of the inner struggle in all its nuances.[20]

What then was Eisenstein's solution? It is contained in the following:

> The camera had to penetrate "inside" Clyde. Aurally and visually must be set down the feverish *race* of *thoughts,* intermittently with the outer actuality—the boat, the girl sitting

opposite him, his own actions. The form of the "inner monologue" was born.[21]

We can get a better idea of just how Eisenstein intended
to handle the stream of consciousness material, or inner monologue, by examining some of the numerous notes and sketches
that he made in order to help formulate the *montage* sequences; the following is a description by Eisenstein himself
of these numerous jottings:

> What wonderful sketches those montage lists were!
> Like thought, they would sometimes proceed with visual
> images. With sound. Synchronized or non-synchronized. Then
> as sounds. Formless. Or with sound images: with objectively
> representational sounds . . .
> Then suddenly, definite intellectually formulated words—
> as "intellectual" and dispassionate as pronounced words. With
> a black screen, a rushing imageless visuality.
> Then in passionate disconnected speech. Nothing but nouns.
> Or nothing but verbs. Then interjections. With zigzags of
> aimless shapes, whirling along with these in synchronization.
> Then racing visual images over complete silence.
> Then linked with polyphonic sounds. Then polyphonic
> images. Then both at once.
> Then interpolated into the outer course of action, then
> interpolating elements of the outer action into the inner
> monologue.
> As if presenting inside the characters the inner play, the
> conflict of doubts, the explosions of passion, the voice of reason,
> rapidly or in slow-motion, marking the different rhythms of
> one and the other and, at the same time, contrasting with the
> almost complete absence of outer action: a feverish inner
> debate behind the stony mask of the face.[22]

At the very least, this proposed *montage* material for *An
American Tragedy* indicates that Eisenstein intended to make
a motion picture that would have been a unique and exciting
experience for the viewer; unfortunately, however, the project
never progressed beyond the treatment stage. It is indeed
ironical that the most imaginative application of the psycho-

logical principles of stream of consciousness in the first sixty years of the history of cinema should be found in a film that was never actually made.* (In a later chapter we shall see an even more revolutionary rendering of stream of consciousness in a film made by Michelangelo Antonioni [*La Notte*].)

Before we end our discussion, we should at least call attention to the 1967 film adaptation of James Joyce's novel *Ulysses*, perhaps the most famous stream of consciousness novel ever written. Unfortunately, though, this adaptation by Joseph Strick proved rather disappointing; there was little new in the way stream of consciousness was handled. While faithfully depicting the flow of the novel's stream-of-consciousness material—primarily through direct cuts—Strick's film generally resorted to the use of voice-over for the depiction of the qualitative aspects of consciousness; thus, there was little attempt at providing *visual* images that corresponded to, or evoked, Joyce's masterful verbal images.

---

* Two rather inferior adaptations of Dreiser's novel were subsequently made, however: the first (1931) was directed by the late Josef von Sternberg; the second (1951) went under the title *A Place in the Sun* and was directed by George Stevens.

9

Existentialism and the Anti-Hero in Cinema

The topic of this chapter is probably best exemplified by the first two features of French director Jean-Luc Godard—*Breathless* (*A bout de souffle,* 1959) and *Le Petit Soldat* (1960) —with the inner logic and philosophical roots of these two films being derived from the same two general sources —the American *film noir,* or crime film, and existentialist philosophy.

Existentialism

As a philosophy, existentialism enjoyed its greatest popularity in Europe immediately after the Second World War; undoubtedly influenced by the horrors of that conflict, the major tenets of this philosophy were primarily derived from the post-war writings of Jean-Paul Sartre (in France) and Karl Jaspers (in Germany). Essentially, post-war existentialism emphasized the meaninglessness of the universe, the arbitrary nature of the world, the unintelligibility of life and the necessity to *act* in a way that would tend to make our lives both *meaningful* and *intelligible*. It is no secret that many French existentialist writers—and especially Sartre—were profoundly influenced by the tough crime novels of such American writers of the Thirties as Dashiell Hammett, Raymond Chandler and James M. Cain; it should not be surprising, therefore, to learn that a certain sympathy toward existentialism was uncovered in the film adaptations of these crime novels (made predominately in Hollywood during the Forties) by Jean-Luc Godard and his fellow critics on the magazine *Cahiers du Cinéma* during the Fifties. The importance of this discovery to Godard's subsequent work as a filmmaker can best be gauged by noting that his first serious study of cinema began with the American film.

The American film noir

The most celebrated example of these quasi-existentialist American crime films was *The Maltese Falcon,* adapted in 1940 from a novel by Dashiell Hammett, and which starred Humphrey Bogart; this film was to serve as the prototype for an entire *genre* of American motion pictures that came to be identified by French critics as *films noirs* ("black films"). In their extensive study of this *genre,* two French critics, Raymond Borde and Etienne Chaumenton, made the following pertinent observations:[1] first, the *film noir* is chiefly identified by the presence of crime considered from the point of view of the criminal; secondly, the *film noir* is unique in its treatment of morality in that there is no clear-cut distinction shown between good and evil; thirdly, the "heros" of these films are generally dubious characters such as tough private eyes or occasionally an ex-G.I., but always someone at home in dealing with the underworld; and fourthly, the main theme of these films is concerned with violence—violence of a brutal, vengeful, psychopathic nature. The "heroines" of these films are also quite unique: they follow an ambiguous path and seem to specialize in duplicity and betrayal. Another important characteristic of the *film noir*, which Borde and Chaumenton pointed out, was that the action and plots of these films are often confused; the spectator is disoriented. For example, in *The Big Sleep*, made in 1946 from Raymond Chandler's novel of the same name, there is even one murder that the author was not quite sure about—Was it murder, or was it suicide?

To summarize: the main points to keep in mind when we examine Godard's first two feature films are that for their occasional meaninglessness, arbitrariness, unintelligibility and emphasis on the necessity to act, we should attribute the influence of existentialism; for their emphasis on crime, confusion, ambiguous morality, duplicity and violence, we should attribute the influence of the *film noir*.

Breathless *and* Le Petit Soldat

In *Breathless* Godard takes the American *film noir* one step further. Here, Michel Poiccard, the film's protagonist and undisputable anti-hero, has almost no redeeming characteristics whatsoever. A petty criminal who apparently lacks any moral values or concrete motivation, Michel is hunted down by the police for the murder of a highway patrolman (no immoral act or piece of callous behavior is too unthinkable for him: he steals automobiles on impulse; he even steals from a girl-friend who has just given him money; and when his American mistress informs him that he is responsible for her pregnancy, he tells her to be more careful next time). But what is even more appalling, Michel cares less about himself: he is apparently unconcerned about escaping from the police; his attempts at a "get-away" seem half-hearted. And when his girl-friend tells him that she has betrayed him to the police, he is not particularly worried, and makes no attempt to escape, allowing himself to be shot down in the street by his pursuers.

Though Michel apparently lacks any concrete motivation, he does possess tremendous vitality. He lives each moment for the present, unconcerned about its connection with the past, of its consequences for the future. Whether he steals a car or performs in bed with a girl, he does so with gusto. Michel may be just a "punk" attempting to imitate Humphrey Bogart—which he overtly does in one scene—but, as imaginatively played by Jean-Paul Belmondo, he is a "punk" with style. Though Michel's complete moral lassitude and failure to act decisively may not make him an existential hero in the true sense of the term, Godard's film, with its focus on individual actions in the midst of an almost totally meaningless existence, bears the unmistakable existentialist imprint. In making *Breathless,* Godard believed that he was making a conventional gangster film; however, he later realized that he had not in fact made a realistic film—a *Scarface,* for instance—but an *Alice in Wonderland* instead.[2] In his next feature, *Le Petit Soldat,* Godard would once again attempt to make a realistic film; that is, to deal with the concrete.

In *Le Petit Soldat* ("The Little Soldier"), Godard presents the anti-hero in a still more negative light. This time he casts in the role of the protagonist an actor who is notably unappealing, definitely lacking the style and personal magnetism of a Jean-Paul Belmondo (although this actor, Michel Subor, intelligently portrays his part). In departing even further from the tradition of the *film noir,* this protagonist is self-conscious, reflective and a pseudo-intellectual.

The film begins as the main character, Bruno Forestier, is about to cross the Swiss border into France. He tells us, "For me, the time for action is over—I have aged. The time for reflection begins." From the very beginning there is an extremely important difference between the Bruno of *Le Petit Soldat* and the Michel of *Breathless:* Michel was a man of instinct, caring little about the meaning and consequences of his acts; Bruno, however, must reflect on everything—his life is a constant, albeit unsuccessful, search for meaning. Gradually, the pieces of the film fall together. We learn that Bruno is a deserter from the French army who has been living and working in Geneva as a correspondent for a French news agency. As an avocation he has been working for a French right-wing terrorist organization that has been operating in Switzerland throughout the Algerian war against their Arab counterparts—the FLN (the story is supposed to take place in 1958).*

Bruno's terrorist comrades, having grown suspicious of his activities and doubting his courage and loyalty, order him to assassinate a Swiss radio commentator who has been extremely sympathetic to the FLN in his broadcasts; Bruno refuses—for no other reason than that he feels it would be a defeat. If he does not go through with the assassination, his comrades warn, they will retaliate; but Bruno will not be intimidated. The terrorists, however, make good their threat: they implicate Bruno with the Swiss police by "framing" him in a phoney automobile accident.

Bruno now realizes that all resistance against his former friends is futile and agrees to carry out the assassination, a decision that he himself acknowledges as cowardly. Bruno's half-hearted attempts at murder fail to come off, however, and he is pursued by both the French terrorists and the Arabs, the latter of whom catch up with him first and take him to an apartment to be interrogated. The Arabs suggest that Bruno work for them, but when he asks them for some money in advance they refuse; so Bruno tells them "to get lost." The Arabs then torture him with ironic brutality: they cannot understand why Bruno refuses to give them the infor-

---

* We learn all this from the voice-over (*narratage*) spoken by Bruno throughout the film.

mation that they seek, since he has already admitted to them that he has no ideals. After having bravely resisted the torture, Bruno tries to commit suicide but fails.

Finally, however, he manages to effect a miraculous escape and goes to hide out at his girl-friend's apartment, at which time she confesses that she has been working for the Arabs; Bruno forgives her, and they make plans to escape together to Brazil. In exchange for two diplomatic passports, Bruno proposes to give his former terrorist friends the address of the Arabs who tortured him. The French terrorists take the information, and later tell him that they checked out the address but found no Arabs living there; Bruno is given an ultimatum—kill the Swiss commentator or there will be no passports. As Bruno sets out once again to perform the assassination, the French kidnap his girl-friend in order to obtain the new address of the Arab agents—and it is only after he has killed the Swiss that Bruno finds out she was tortured and murdered by her abductors. As Bruno arranges his flight from Switzerland, he leaves us with a final thought about the possible meaning of the events that he has just recounted: "Only one thing was left to me: learn not to be bitter. But I was happy, because I had a lot of time in front of me."

Rarely in the history of the cinema has there been a character as negative as the Bruno of Jean-Luc Godard's *Le Petit Soldat*. Early in the film Bruno tells us, "Up to now my story has been simple. It's about a fellow without ideals."[3] A secret agent without conviction, Bruno does not even know why he has so bravely resisted torture, only to attempt suicide: "Why did I want to kill myself?" he asks himself, "I would have done better to tell them what they wanted."[4] Even though Bruno seldom knows the answers to the questions that he asks, he is still committed to continue asking them. For, as he so astutely observes, "Perhaps after all asking questions is more important than finding answers."[5]

It is toward the end of the film that Bruno finally gives us a little insight into the reasons behind his actions: "If you stay quietly doing nothing, you are cursed just because you are doing nothing," he says. "So, we do things without conviction. . ."[6] Trapped in a meaningless existence, the only way for Bruno to keep his sanity is to embrace both love and life, the only two things that he can accept on pure faith, without endless questioning.

Le Petit Soldat is noteworthy not only for its unusual characterization of Bruno but also for its treatment of violence. The *film noir* had always been predicated on violence, but as we have already mentioned, this violence was always of an intensely brutal, vengeful, psychopathic nature. In *Le Petit Soldat,* however, violence becomes detached, dehumanized and, as a consequence, utterly meaningless. One of Bruno's friends in the film, commenting on a terrorist bombing, says, "Kill a fellow in the back, okay . . . but with a revolver, at least, or a knife, but not with a bomb. . . . It's true, killing a man from a distance, I think it's dishonest."[7] But the logic of terrorism is not a moral one, and, as Godard shows us, the tactics of both the Right and the Left are indistinguishable. Made at a time when France was deeply embroiled in the Algerian war, it is not very surprising that the French censors kept *Le Petit Soldat* from being publicly shown for three years. The ironical thing is, however, that in being political—that is, in making a film on a political subject—Godard is really being apolitical; politics in this film is depicted as something completely irrelevant, if not totally meaningless.

Aesthetically, *Le Petit Soldat*—and, for that matter, also *Breathless*—suffers because Godard seems to be presenting his protagonist as a postulate instead of as a character in a vain attempt to push his (Godard's) existentialist philosophy to the limit of—or perhaps beyond—its logical implications; in short, the film is much too contrived. Evidently Godard recognized this fault, for he has subsequently said that he now tries to come a little closer to his characters, "not to judge them or to hold them up as models (either good or bad), and try to keep from making them into types or prototypes that simply correspond to ideas."[8] Another aesthetic flaw in *Le Petit Soldat*, dealt with in the chapter on dramaturgy, is that the character of Bruno is so negative and odious to most people, and the actor who portrays him so lacking in personal magnetism, that audiences fail to closely identify with him and thus lose interest in the film. However, this may not be so much a defect in the film as a defect in most audiences: readers have long accepted negative characters and anti-heros in literature and not demanded that they be able to identify with them; so why cannot the same attitude be adopted toward film? Godard's film, however, was coolly received by both the critics and movie audiences when it was finally released for distribution (1963).

Whatever the merits of *Le Petit Soldat*—and I, for one, believe that there are many—Godard was to make a very important discovery concerning his approach to reality in cinema: "The closer I drew to the concrete the more theatrical my work became."[9] Never again would Godard approach reality in the very same way.

10

Federico Fellini and the Psychoanalytic Technique in Film

The fullest expression in cinema of Sigmund Freud's psychoanalytic theories (some of which have already been discussed) is most readily to be found in the films of Federico Fellini. While not the profoundest of filmmakers working in cinema today, Fellini is certainly one of the most fascinating; even though his films sometimes miss their mark, they never fail to dazzle: what they may lack in substance, they more than compensate for in their pure visual beauty and splendor. Perhaps for the key to understanding this special awe that Fellini's films inspire, we must look back to his childhood; for Fellini the adult film director is not too different from Fellini the somewhat mischievous child, who, at the age of twelve, ran away from home to join the circus. "I have a complex about being a little schoolboy—intimidated but somewhat naughty," Fellini has said about himself;[1] indeed, his films seem to reflect this—with all the tawdry spectacle of a three-ring circus and the charm and irreverence of a child's mind.

Fellini's first job in films was that of a scriptwriter (he collaborated with Roberto Rossellini on the scenario for *Open City*), and his first scripts were written during, and definitely within the context of, the neo-realist period in Italian cinema that flowered immediately after the Second World War. But "reality," as we have seen it defined and employed by Zavattini and other Italian neo-realist film-makers, was too restrictive for Fellini: he chose to go on and explore a world on film that perhaps can best be described as more "*sur*real" than "real."

Of Fellini's earlier films (he co-directed his first, *Variety Lights* [*Luci del varietà*] in 1950), the most important is un-questionably *La strada* (1954), a somber story, told in nat-uralistic tones, of the pathetic relationship between a brutish itinerant sideshow strongman, Zampanò (excellently acted by Anthony Quinn), and a simple-minded waif called Gel-somina (played by Fellini's wife, Giulietta Masina); Fellini calls this film "the complete catalogue of my entire mythical world, a dangerous representation of my identity without precautions."[2] However, it was not until 1959, when he made the notorious *La dolce vita*, that a world-wide recogni-tion was finally assured Fellini; this film, which reflects his somewhat ambivalent pre-occupation with the splendor and decadence of modern-day Rome, both shocked and fascinated —somewhat voyeuristically—filmgoers throughout the world with its sumptuous spectacle and bizarre sequences. Here we see for the first time Fellini's complete mastery of his medium —his fluid use of the moving camera and, in the precision of his casting for the bit parts, his awareness of the expressive-ness and plasticity of the human face. Despite its enormous breadth and sweep, however, *La dolce vita* never actually rises above the level of a bizarre spectacle—although Fellini vainly strived to raise it to a level of profundity—primarily because the film's protagonist, a morally-confused journalist played by Marcello Mastroianni, is not sufficiently strong as a point of focus to counterbalance the pervasive permissiveness (for the period).

Fellini's Method of Working

Since one of the avowed purposes of this book is to study the creative process of filmmaking, especially as it relates to the screenplay, a brief examination of how Fellini goes about making a film—from conception to completion—would be highly informative for our purpose. Fellini is a filmmaker who has gained the reputation of never knowing what he is going to do next, of being constantly in a state of crisis— both creative and personal—and of relying almost completely on improvisation; indeed, he openly admits to "working on the irrational bases of sensitivity," of which there "is nothing concrete, nothing that can be calculated, nothing foreseeable."[3] However, this is a somewhat distorted picture of the way in which he actually works; contrary to what most people believe, or what he himself may say about his *modus operandi*, his films are in fact very carefully worked out by himself and several scriptwriters (which have included, in the past, Tullio Pinelli, Brunello Rondi and Ennio Flaiano), even though, as he himself admits, his films may not be "as neat and precise as the design of a crystal," and tend to be predominately told "in sweeping cadences."[4]

Let us examine Fellini's method of working in greater detail. The idea for a Fellini film, no matter how obscure its source, always finds its first embodiment in the form of a story—perhaps the most important stage of the film's development for this director. (Of his early work in films Fellini has said that he was only interested in the telling of a story, paying little or no attention to cinematic technique or visual elements[5]—an attitude that he has obviously changed, but not so greatly, for Fellini is still the story teller, the *raconteur* of dazzling and magnificent tales.)

Out of the story evolves the screenplay, which as was indicated above, is usually the product of Fellini's collaboration with several other writers. Finally, when he feels "the screenplay isn't sufficient, that it is useless to carry on further on a literary level,"[6] Fellini opens up his office and begins calling in people so that he may have hundreds of faces pass before him, which he describes as "a kind of ceremony to create an atmosphere, one of the many and certainly not the most important."[7] Thus begins the casting for a Fellini film, probably one of the most important elements that contribute to his particular kind of cinematic genius. "For my pictures I go in search of expressive faces that can say everything when they first appear on the screen," he has said;[8] "Faces are my words."[9] And if a filmmakers' vocabulary were to be judged solely on the number and distinctiveness of the bit-players in his films, a film by Fellini could be likened to a cinematic Roget's *Thesaurus*.

It is not the screenplay that Fellini finds the most crucial element of the production but the *atmosphere* in which he creates. As he has been quoted as saying:

> The real work isn't making a choice of character before or after, or deciding what he has to say. That decision will come, and it will be the right one, if you have been able to create a vital atmosphere in which something might be born. Everything can come together to create this atmosphere, which first surrounds you as an individual and then the set on which you work.[10]

For Fellini, who has been fascinated with circuses and variety shows since childhood, it is not at all surprising that he is at his creative best when the atmosphere in which he works most closely resembles the chaos of a circus that is being set up and dismantled, *ad infinitum*.

At a certain point, when he feels that he has had enough

of the parade of people passing before him in his office, Fellini begins the screen tests, which he calls "the definite phase of the ceremony. At this point I know that in a short time I have to begin the film."[11] Thus, the shooting of a Fellini film is about to begin, and, concomitantly, the screenplay—which Fellini believes begins with the idea and ends with the first copy, "even the first showing of the film"[12]—is about to undergo extensive revisions; "Everything can be changed; and everything is, in fact, born, not respecting what you have prepared. At this point, it is pointless to remain faithful to steps you have made, to the choices made the day before yesterday, to something written five months before."[13] And so, as the shooting progresses, scenes and characters are substituted, situations are enriched and dialogue is changed —"Often, while I shoot, I prefer to have the actors recite numbers rather than sentences written months before, which I feel to be dated and out of place."[14] (New dialogue is then written and dubbed* in after the shooting is completed.) The reader must not gain the impression, however, that because Fellini reserves the right to make extensive changes in the screenplay after the preliminary stage, he does not have any concrete idea of how the film will turn out; as he himself has said, "I believe I have the internal rhythm of the sequence in mind well before shooting begins. In this I am very faithful to my first conceptions: when I begin to see a scene in a certain way, I make no more changes."[15]

Enough of Fellini's method of working; let us now return to the real topic of this chapter, "The Psychoanalytic Technique in Film," and see how Fellini incorporates it in two of his most extraordinary films.

---

* *Dubbing* is a process by which an actor's voice is recorded after a film has been shot and substituted for his or another actor's voice that was recorded during shooting. This process is sometimes referred to as *postsynchronization,* and is commonly employed in all Fellini films as well as in many European productions.

8½

In 1963, Fellini made his one true film masterpiece to date (excluding, perhaps, *La Strada*), 8½ (*Otto e mezzo*); in this highly autobiographical film about a middle-aged director (played by Marcello Mastroianni) suffering from a creative block, who apparently tries vainly to make his eighth-and-a-half film (prior to this, Fellini had made seven features and two episodes which approximate to half a film, thus the significance of the title), Fellini was finally to find an apt vehicle for his burgeoning cinematic talents.

Earlier in this book we mentioned that free-association was a principle that sometimes governs the direction and flow of thought material in a stream of consciousness—with the more removed or relaxed the influence of the will on the mind, the greater the degree of free-association. Fellini employs this same principle in the structuring of 8½, but in a manner more closely identified with Freud's psychoanalytic techniques. These, in brief summary, are as follows (see also Chapter Eight): in certain mental states during which the action of the will is reduced or absent altogether, certain other factors or forces (e.g. unresolved internal conflicts which arise primarily in childhood) that exist in the subconscious may, on the other hand, heavily influence the direction and flow of the thoughts in the stream of consciousness (i.e. their juxtaposition and nature); thus, in such instances, the associations that make up the stream of consciousness are not actually "free" at all—and, therefore, by analyzing the "stream" during such mental states, one may possibly uncover the origin and identity of these unresolved subconscious conflicts where they do exist.

In 8½, however, Fellini attempts to uncover the unresolved conflicts—some conscious, other unconscious—of his main character (Guido), not by filming one continuous stream of consciousness from the mind of the character but by selecting only a few (actually eleven) dreams, flashbacks (i.e. memories) and fantasies from the "stream" which yield insight providing associations into Guido's psyche (and perhaps Fellini's also).* Thus, Professor Gessner saw the structure of this film as being twofold: "The narrative line concerning the frustrations over the pending film production and a parallel line composed of flashback dreams and psychic fantasies, meant to explore the childhood motivations or adult escapes."[16]

The narrative line

Let us first examine the straight, linear development of Fellini's film.† 8½, like *Wild Strawberries* to which it is closely related,†† also begins with a nightmare dream sequence: Guido, while driving in his car, is caught in a monumental traffic jam. Obsessed with the desire to escape from the confines of his car, he glides through its roof and soars high into the sky, bound only by a rope tied to his foot, which is held by a man on a beach. Finally, the man with the rope pulls him to earth in a dizzying spin to the sea. After this dream sequence—which signifies, perhaps, impending disaster—we find Guido in bed at a health spa, attended by two doctors: he is suffering from some kind of—imaginary?

---

* In an earlier chapter we noted that, technically, dreams—which actually belong to the state of sleep (or the unconscious)—are not part of the stream of consciousness; however, in 8½, Fellini does not include dreams as part of his protagonist's modified stream of consciousness.

† This treatment by me of 8½ has suffered because no published edition of Fellini's screenplay has yet been made available in English. In place of a published screenplay, however, I found Deena Boyer's book *The Two Hundred Days of 8½* (trans. by Charles Lam Markmann, New York, The Macmillan Company, 1964), which contains a synopsis of Fellini's original scenario, an immense aid. Miss Boyer, who was Fellini's "on-set press officer" for 8½, kept a day-by-day account of how the production proceeded, including many interesting and pertinent anecdotes—some of which I have included in this discussion.

†† Fellini himself has said that he liked *Wild Strawberries* very much and found it very close to his own temperament.[17]

—illness, and is visited by an intellectual writer (called Carini in the original scenario, but later changed to Daumier during the dubbing) whom Guido wants as a collaborator on the forthcoming film. Having set up his production office at the spa, Guido is visited by his producer, actresses, extras, etc.; everyone wants him to tell them what the film is about and, especially the actresses and their agents, just what their parts are going to be. Guido, however, refuses to make any pronouncements—does he really know what he is going to do? is he just stalling for time? We wonder.

From his conversations with the writer Daumier, who has read the script and contemptuously disapproves of it, we are given the impression that the film Guido is about to embark on is based on "tender" childhood recollections which are concerned with his Catholic upbringing. However, from what his producer says, and also from what we can deduce from one of the sets under construction—a huge rocket and its launching platform—we are given the impression that Guido is going to make some sort of science fiction film (see below for a further explanation of Guido's film).

While resting and (supposedly) working on his film at the spa, Guido—as if asking for trouble—sends for both his wife and mistress. His mistress (Carla) is overtly sexual, and happily indulges all his erotic whims, while his wife (Luisa), a mature, strikingly attractive woman, is constantly disapproving of his conduct. Naturally enough, Guido's irrational impulse has the inevitable consequences: his wife discovers the presence of his mistress—something that Guido has made only a feeble effort to hide—and a marital flare-up promptly ensues. Later, during the projection of the screen tests for Guido's film—tests to be used to fill roles based on all the people who have figured importantly in his life—Luisa storms out of the screening room, having taken offense at one of the parts being auditioned for—herself. As she leaves, she tells her husband that as far as she is concerned he can go straight to Hell. The projection of the screen tests continues, how-

ever, and as it does, Claudia, an attractive young actress, secretly arrives to discuss the details of the role she is to play
in Guido's film (Claudia is played by the same actress—
Claudia Cardinale—who has previously appeared throughout
the film as a vision he apparently associates with innocence
and purity, and, as a corollary, his ultimate salvation). Guido
and Claudia sneak out of the screening room together and
go for a ride in her car. During this ride, Guido tells her the
subject of the film: It is, he says, the story of a man in love
with neither his wife nor mistress; he is, instead, in love with
a young, pure girl—Claudia herself?—whom the man thinks
could set his mixed-up life straight again.* Guido asks Claudia whether she herself could fall in love with such a man
and give up everything for him. She answers forthrightly
that she could never love a man who has proven to be so
callous to the two women in his life, for such a man has shown
himself incapable of love. Guido admits that she is perhaps
right, and that there probably will be no film either.

The next day Guido's producer drags him to a press con-

---

* From Deena Boyer's book, I have pieced together what I believe to
have been the original concept of Fellini's film—which ultimately became,
in part, the concept for Guido's proposed work. A man—at first just any
middle-aged professional man—goes to a spa to take a cure and begins to
reflect on his life. There he meets the daughter of a museum watchman,
a young, innocent girl in whom he believes he can find salvation through
loving. The girl agrees to give up everything and go away with him; but
he, incapable of a lasting relationship, leaves the spa without her. Later,
this "professional" evolved into a screenwriter who is going through a
crisis in both his professional and private life. He is commissioned to write
a script, and in doing so, imagines a sequence in which mankind, including
the Catholic Church, abandons the earth in a gigantic spaceship; this
sequence is supposed to reflect on his own crisis, but on a much broader
basis: mankind, like himself, must abandon earth and start again someplace
else. Finally, Fellini turned his protagonist into a director, with the previous
versions amalgamated into the film that his protagonist is trying to make,
the sequence of the spaceship serving as the climax of his own (Guido's)
picture, based on his own crisis. In the final version, the daughter of the
museum watchman evolved into the role of Claudia, the actress Guido selected
to play the heroine (of Fellini's earlier version). Such a story-line is rightly
confusing, for 8½ is actually a film within a film within a film . . . ad
infinitum.

ference held at the set for the rocket launching platform;
Guido is given an ultimatum by his producer, to face the
press and begin shooting the film or he will ruin Guido's
career. Reluctantly, Guido faces the press, but has nothing to
say. Then, in fantasy, he dreams that he commits suicide, and
thus ends everything. Back in reality we see the rocket set
being dismantled. Daumier, the writer, tells Guido that he
has made the right decision in abandoning the film, because
it would probably have ruined his career—and, besides, what
could be a greater achievement for an artist than to create
nothing and silence.* In fantasy, Guido brings together all
the people in his life, and all the characters in the film, for
one grand circus finale in which he says to them (in a voice-
over) that his big mistake in life was to fight instead of to
accept them. His wife, dressed in white, is also there for the
finale. She tells Guido that she has been wrong in not accepting him for what he is; if he will help her, Luisa tells her
husband she will try to start over again with him. Thus the
film ends; Guido has ostensibly worked out his personal
problems—at least in fantasy.†

---

* The rationale behind the character of Daumier is interesting. It is quite
obvious that no collaboration between this stuffy, pedantic intellectual and
the very impulsive and flamboyant Guido could have even been remotely
conceivable. Why then did Guido (or Fellini) choose him? In the case of
Guido, it is obvious that Daumier serves as a hair shirt—a kind of penance—
whose criticisms Guido never once intended to pay heed to; this is made
all the easier for Guido by the fact that the critic himself has such an
obnoxious personality. In the case of Fellini, Daumier was no doubt meant
to provide a foil for his protagonist. However, some critics have said that
the real purpose of Daumier was to make the very points against Guido's
film, and in essence Fellini's film (e.g. that these tender childhood memories lack any real substance or content, etc.), that the film critics would—
and eventually did—make before they themselves had the opportunity.
Deena Boyer mentions that during the dubbing Fellini decided to elevate
Daumier to the height of a symbol: the apologist for a school of criticism
that stands for nullity—a school which believes that the only real artistic
perfection is to be found in nothingness (e.g. the blank page, etc.).

† Fellini actually shot two endings for his film: the one described above,
which was ultimately used, and a second version, which was indicated in the
original scenario. In the latter, instead of having all the people in Guido's
life and the film gathered together for a circus finale, they are now seated

Flashbacks and fantasies

Of the eleven flashbacks and dream fantasies to be found in *8½*, only three actually shed light on the subconscious conflicts that have molded Guido's personality; the remaining eight are primarily sexual fantasies and noteworthy more for their bizarreness than for any possible hidden meanings. Of the three that do provide important insight into the personality of the protagonist, the first occurs just after Guido has had sexual relations with his mistress; it is a dream fantasy in which Guido's mother takes him for a visit to the family tomb where he talks to his dead father, who complains to his son about how small and cramped his final resting place is; at the end, Guido tenderly kisses his mother, who suddenly turns into a woman that—we are later to find out—is his wife. The meaning of this first psychic association is very clear; it expresses Guido's guilty feelings about sex, while at the same time pointing to the existence of a confused mother-son-wife conflict or relationship. It is during the performance of a clairvoyant that the second psychological insight is gained: Guido is transported back to his childhood (*via* a flashback) and is lovingly bathed, fondled and put to bed by his female relatives; this tender childhood memory undoubtedly reveals the origin of Guido's subconscious desire for all the women—both real and imaginary—in his adult life to both devote their lives and pay continual homage to him (it is significant that in a later sexual fantasy, Guido imagines that these same women now constitute a harem of which he himself is the master and in the very same

in a railway dining car (as part of another dream fantasy) along with Guido and his wife. The meaning of both endings, however, is identical: Guido's total acceptance of his present and past life, and all the people in it (although in this second version the imminence of a separation between Guido and his wife is emphasized considerably more). Deena Boyer reports that Fellini made his final choice between the two endings solely on the basis of showmanship—a choice which, she tells us, was unanimously endorsed by all those who worked on the production.

farmhouse where he was lovingly fondled as a child). The final piece of psychological insight is triggered by Guido's glimpse of an obese woman's thigh; this is juxtaposed to a flashback of a childhood incident in which Guido is apprehended and punished by the priests of his parochial school after paying a prostitute to dance obscenely: an association that is clearly meant to express the subconscious conflict (although possibly conscious conflict also) between his strict Catholic upbringing and his pre-occupation with sex—a conflict that we sense has remained with Guido throughout his entire adult life.

In *Wild Strawberries* we pointedly asked the questions "Does Isak Borg gain any insight into himself through his dreams?" and if he does, "Is he able to resolve any of the internal conflicts that his dreams provide evidence of?" Although we had to answer "No" to each of these, we did note that Isak had perhaps mellowed somewhat by the film's end. In *8½* we must ask similar questions: "Does Guido gain any insight into himself through his dreams, memories and fantasies?" and if so, "Is he able to use this newly-gained knowledge to resolve his inner conflicts concerning religion and sex, as they currently affect his life both personally and professionally?" The answer to the first question must be an unqualified "Yes," since Guido himself admits the possession of such insight at the film's end;* however, as to the second question, the answer would appear to be "No"—but let us examine this particular one a little further before drawing any final conclusions.

I think that we can immediately dismiss any notion that Guido changes or will change with respect to his personal life. It is certainly doubtful that his wife will ever accept Guido's philandering or that he will give up his mistress.

---

* According to the story line of the film, Guido does gain this insight, or at least admits that he does. However, this does not mean that it is at all plausible according to standard psychoanalytic technique for Guido to gain such an insight on his own—that is, without professional psychiatric help.

However, in regard to the removal of Guido's very enigmatic "creative block," there seems to be some indication that progress has or will be made. But just what is Guido's creative block? We know that he has written the script for his proposed film—or at least a first draft of it—and that he is already involved in the casting. Yet Guido bemoans the fact that he lacks "poetic inspiration" and that he wants to say everything but has nothing to say. Notwithstanding all this fine talk about an artistic crisis, we are sometimes given the impression that Guido is insincere, that this is all part of a ritual—a ritual he goes through before the start of every film. It would appear, then, that Guido needs not "poetic inspiration" but someone to fire him to start the film—something that his producer tries but fails to do. What, then, is Guido's problem—is this just the calm before the creative storm, with Guido evoking as much pity as he is able, or is he actually on the verge of a disaster?

Deena Boyer reports that Fellini told her (shortly after shooting began) that Guido is really hoping one minute to the next that somehow he will find a way out and determine just where it is that he and his film are going, but ultimately fails in this endeavor and falls flat on his face, with everything disintegrating around him. However, Fellini's pronouncements about Guido's "creative block" may be a little deceptive and may have actually changed during the course of the shooting; so let us now examine Guido's *impasse* from still another point of view.

It is essential that we be aware that this was Fellini's problem also. We know that he, like Guido, started off on the wrong foot in making his film; however, Fellini eventually regained the right track.* The question is, Will Guido? Before we answer that, however, let us examine both Fellini's

---

* Miss Boyer tells us that the final draft of Fellini's script was not completed until a few days after filming began and was continually being revised during the course of the production.

and Guido's creative problem more closely, since they are basically the same.

"I wanted to make an honest picture, without lies," Guido confesses; but how did he first attempt to do this? The same way as Fellini: by making a film in which his protagonist—really himself—instead of reflecting on and facing up to his personal crisis directly, abstracts it—that is, reflects on it on a much broader basis: e.g. mankind attempting to leave the earth in a gigantic spaceship in order to start over again. And, as pre-production on the two films progressed—Fellini's and Guido's—both became more autobiographical and consequently less abstract and more honest. Thus, the ridiculous rocket-launching platform in both films is only a crutch—a crutch that Fellini in the end was able to discard, and, hopefully, Guido also.

At the end of her book, Deena Boyer dismisses Fellini's earlier pessimistic pronouncements on Guido's future and says that he (Guido), now at peace with all the people in his life, will continue to make his film. Yes, Guido will make his film, just as Fellini; but only if he has the courage, as had Fellini, to face up to his life and the people in it, and not seek bizarre and escapist abstractions of his problems.

8½ is a film about a man's complete psyche (while *Wild Strawberries* was limited to only a man's dreams); in 1963 it both confused and dazzled audiences with the unorthodox way it jumped from past, present and fantasy without warning (i.e. no traditional "rippled" dissolves or "soft" focus), providing wry, sometimes erotic, glimpses of one of cinema's most fertile imaginations.

Juliet of the Spirits

In his next feature—his first in color—*Juliet of the Spirits* (*Giulietta degli spiriti*, 1965), Fellini further developed his use of the psychoanalytic technique (including free association) in what has been contemptuously referred to by some critics as a female companion-piece to *8½*. An artistic venture fraught with many conceptual difficulties, not the least of which was Fellini's avowed desire to make a film about his wife Giulietta Masina (who plays the film's protagonist) —"I felt that my desire to use the cinema as an instrument to penetrate certain areas of reality could find the perfect guide in Giulietta"[18]—*Juliet of the Spirits* is a veritable and visual Pandora's box, continually brimming over with bizarre colors and dazzling cinematic techniques. It was not only Fellini's desire to make a film about his wife, however, that imperilled the whole undertaking from the start, but also his avowed intention of making a film about women in general: "The intention of the film . . . is to restore to woman her true independence, her indisputable and inalienable dignity," he has said about *Juliet of the Spirits*.[19] That is not to say that Fellini was unaware of the inherent risks in making such a film, for he openly admitted that "to undertake to speak calmly and clearly about a woman is almost impossible for a man. If I have faced this and continue to face it, it is because a story-teller has the right to speak about everything, regardless of his inadequacy."[20]

But it is in the telling of the story, and not so much in its subject matter—"Woman"—that the basic aesthetic problem of *Juliet of the Spirits* (which at times appears to oscillate between a simple story, filled with pathos, and an incredible "non-stop" phantasmagoria) lies; perhaps, in the following statement, Fellini himself has best expressed the exact nature of this problem:

> I realize that the film could annoy those who distrust symbols and perhaps delight those who look for symbols everywhere. Although the film lends itself to esoteric, occult, psychoanalytic interpretations, I would like it to be seen in a simpler light: humane and imaginative. Is it a human commentary, enriched by seductive fantasy? Here, this is the critical problem of the film.[21]

The story line

Despite being a brilliant and colorful *tour-de-force* of cinematic display, *Juliet of the Spirits* is actually structured according to a very simple story. The wife of a successful, middle-aged Italian public relations executive has always had feelings of inferiority and doubts about her self-worth— mainly because she has, since her childhood, allowed herself to be dominated by first her mother and sisters and later her husband and elegant friends. Having grown suspicious of her husband's frequent absences, and at the urging of her sister, Juliet agrees to have her husband put under surveillance by a private detective agency, which in turn furnishes conclusive evidence of her husband's infidelity. Learning that his wife now knows of his affair, Juliet's husband deserts her. Thus, at the end of the film Juliet is left alone to discover her own individuality, a task that will be made much easier now that she has been freed from the oppressive influence of her husband, family and "friends" (and, as we shall shortly see, hallucinations and spirits also) .

Orchestration

I have said that *Juliet of the Spirits* contains a simple story; yet this is not evident from Fellini's use of many ingenious devices and techniques to make the film seem more complex than it really is. The main technique that he relies on is *orchestration,* both of the story and the characters. For example, it is essential for the development of the story that the central conflict (and, in this case, basically an inner one) of Juliet—which, as we have already seen, is a serious assault on her self-worth—be made known to the audience; this is done not just once but many times throughout the film. The first occasion occurs during the very first scene, at a seance held at a dinner party to celebrate Juliet's wedding anniversary; Olaf, a Turkish spirit, has the following message for

Juliet: "Who do you think you are? You're no one to any-body. You don't count, you wretched thing."[22] Her innermost anxiety is made unmistakably clear to us at the film's very beginning through the use of the ingenious device of the occult.

Two scenes later, while at the beach, Juliet comes into the presence for the first time of her next-door neighbor Susy, the beautiful and seductive mistress of a Greek millionaire; Fellini describes her as "an exaggerated, inflated figure—all sex. . . . a kind of enchantress of love, a mistress of eroti-cism," who is meant to be "the incarnation of the humiliated femininity of the protagonist"—a "psychological component" which represents the "neglected and repressed aspect of Juliet."[23] This "repressed aspect" of the protagonist is further developed in the next scene, in which Juliet has a family re-union with her mother and two sisters—all of whom are much taller and more elegantly dressed than herself—and is sternly admonished for not wearing enough make-up.

Several scenes later Juliet's humiliation is orchestrated for us once more, this time at a meeting with a Hindu *fakir* named Bhisma, who, transformed into the spirit of a seduc-tively beautiful woman, tells Juliet: her husband must be her God; she must be the priestess of his cult and try to please him more; women must learn their trade—the prosti-tute's trade? Finally, toward the end of the film, the exact nature of Juliet's internal conflict is *explicitly* revealed to us during a demonstration of psycho-drama, when Dr. Miller, an American psychoanalyst, asks Juliet

> *But what are you afraid of? May I answer? You're afraid of being alone, of being abandoned. You're afraid that your hus-band is going to leave you. And yet you want nothing more than to be left alone; you want your husband to go away. . . . Without Giorgio [Juliet's husband] you'll start to breathe, to live, to become yourself. You think you're afraid. Actually you fear only one thing—to be happy.*[24]

The introduction and development of Juliet's inner conflict is but one example of how Fellini has made this film
appear more complex than it actually is: in this case by the
orchestration of the story. His orchestration of characters was
also mentioned as another example—illustrated not only by
Fellini's already-mentioned precision in the casting of his
films, but also in the way from the original screenplay to the
final film he has in a few instances expanded the dialogue
and business of a character, then added an entirely new
character and split this new dialogue and business between
them: e.g. the addition of another assistant for the Hindu
fakir Bhisma, and the creation of an assistant for the private
detective whom Juliet hires to spy on her husband. Now that
we have seen how Fellini has *presented* and *orchestrated* the
protagonist's central inner conflict by means of the story line
of *Juliet of the Spirits,* let us go on and examine how this
conflict is *explored* and possibly *resolved,* as we did for *8½.*

Flashbacks and fantasies

Here, as in *8½,* the essential medium for the delineation
and resolution of inner conflict is the psyche of the protagonist; the technique for exploring it is again a limited
form of free association—consisting of dreams, flashbacks,
fantasies and hallucinations. The first of these occurs at the
sea-shore (where Juliet also meets Susy for the first time),
a hallucination in which she imagines seeing the landing of
two huge barges that are full of threatening-looking men
and women, naked or nearly naked, along with some dead
animals—all of which represent the dark area of Juliet's
psyche now oppressing her. The next instance occurs during
the scene with Bhisma, in which Juliet associates the spirit
(Iris) who speaks to her through this *fakir* with a hallucination of a beautiful trapeze artist on a white horse (we later
learn that Juliet's grandfather ran off with a beautiful circus

artiste in, what Juliet always believed to be, an airplane) .

The third important psychic association occurs at the studio of one of Juliet's friends, Dolores, who sculpts large erotic statues of healthy, naked bodies, and who tells Juliet (while busily at work on her newest piece of erotica) that "God has the most beautiful body there is. In my work I represent Him that way—physically, corporeally, a hero of the perfect form who I can desire and even take as a lover."[25] Dolores' analogy between God and sex triggers in Juliet's mind a childhood memory of a religious pageant in which she played the role of a martyred saint; in this flashback we see Juliet (as a child) supposedly burned on a metal grating, which is slowly hoisted above the stage of her parochial school, signifying the martyred saint's final ascent to Heaven. However, before the little Juliet can be finally hoisted to the top of the auditorium, her grandfather, who has until now been sitting quietly in the audience, jumps on the stage and disrupts the performance—which he denounces as an "absurdity" as he slowly lowers his stunned little grand-daughter back to the stage. The implied meaning of this association is obvious: the deep conflict between the residue of Juliet's stringent Catholic education and corporeal sexuality (an association similar in purpose to the one in *8½* that contained the flashback of Guido's punishment by the priests in the incident with the prostitute) . Somewhat later in the film, when on the verge of succumbing to a temptation of adultery, Juliet sees a hallucination of this same Christian martyr being burned on the grating, and is then unable to be unfaithful to her husband. (Fellini intended that this image of the saint on the grating symbolize the component of Juliet's psyche which represents masochism and frustration; while Susy, as we have already mentioned, was meant to symbolize the conflicting psychological component representing eroticism and sex) .

The climax of *Juliet of the Spirits,* which contains the resolution of the protagonist's inner conflict, takes place entirely

within her psyche, as was apparently the case in *8½*. Immediately after her husband moves out of their home, probably
never to return again, Juliet finds herself in the midst of a
grotesque and slightly obscene phantasmagoria made up of
her so-called friends dressed in bizarre costumes and the
spirits who have haunted her throughout the film. Outside
the house, Juliet imagines that her grandfather is flying over-
head in an airplane; "I can't come down, I can't land!" he
shouts to her. "It's your fault, Juliet—it all depends on you!"[26]
The phantasmagoria continue to intensify and Juliet turns
to her mother (a hallucination in the form of the elegant but
cold evil queen of children's stories) to ask for help; her
mother, however, remains aloof and fails to answer. Finally,
Juliet opens a small door in her bedroom wall and crawls
through it—against the stern command of her mother; "You
don't frighten me any more," Juliet tells her.[27] Mid-way down
a long, white corridor, Juliet discovers herself as a child,
lying on a grating (just as in the flashback of the religious
pageant) with her hands tied in a position of prayer. Juliet
unties the hands of the child; and with this act the conflict
within her—the central conflict of the film—is finally resolved.
Suddenly all the grotesque members of the phantasmagoria,
now completely motionless, are drawn backwards out of
Juliet's house. Outside, the little Juliet runs to her grandfather who stands beside his airplane as all the members of
the previous hallucinations are pulled away in a large cumbersome wagon. Standing by the front door to her house,
the adult Juliet calls to her grandfather asking him to stay
with her; but he yells to her as his plane is being prepared
for take-off: "Don't hold on to me—you don't need me any
longer. I, too, am an invention of yours; but you are full of
life."[28] Now the little Juliet waves good-bye as her grandfather flies away. The film ends as the adult Juliet walks
towards the woods near her house in brilliant, warm sun-
light; and as she does, she hears voices calling her. "Who are
you?" she asks them; they reply: "True friends, true friends,

true friends."[29] Fellini, in the original screenplay, describes Juliet's mental state as follows:

> *Everything in her is now anchored in peaceful harmony, beyond the mystifying ghosts that have until now besieged her: she is concerned with the daily miracle of simple reality.*
> *Juliet smiles, liberated, at peace.*[30]

It is well worth noting that the final sequences in both the original screenplay and the final version of *Juliet of the Spirits* differ radically: In the finished film we noted that Juliet's inner conflict was resolved by, and her true individuality discovered through, an act of psychic will on her part—Juliet's untying of the hands of her childhood self. However, in the original screenplay Juliet's liberation is not so clearly accomplished by her own efforts, but instead by a *deus ex machina:* Juliet's grandfather descends from a balloon to free her from the phantasmagoria of besieging spirits. This change notwithstanding, the most crucial problem of the film lies in the plausibility of its ending—that is, the ability of Juliet to resolve her internal conflict entirely through her own efforts. Here, the psychoanalytic technique definitely fails, or perhaps more accurately, Fellini's gross over-simplification of it; for the flashbacks, fantasies and hallucinations of the film simply do not provide the protagonist, Juliet, with the means to resolve her inner conflict, unconscious or otherwise: there seems to be little credibility in this sudden act of psychic will from a character that for all her life has passively let herself be acted upon and dominated by others.

One final note on *Juliet of the Spirits.* It was Fellini's second color film (his first was an episode for *Boccaccio '70* [1962]), and according to the director color played a very important role in its construction: the film "is a type of fantasy that is developed through colored illuminations," Fellini has said.[31] Since *Juliet of the Spirits* borders on the surreal, it is not at all surprising that the color scheme Fellini chose

Michel Subor as Bruno Forestier, a secret agent without convictions. With him is Anna Karina as Veronica, his Swiss girl friend in Godard's Le Petit Soldat. *Courtesy: New Yorker Films.*

Giulietta Masina (right) as the oppressed Juliet of Juliet of the Spirits *and Sandra Milo as Susy, her voluptuous neighbor, who symbolizes the heroine's "humiliated femininity." Courtesy of Rizzoli Film, the producer of the film.*

Monica Vitti as the heroine of Antonioni's L'Avventura *and Gabriele Ferzetti as her weak-willed lover. Courtesy: Janus Films.*

Jeanne Moreau as the enigmatic Lidia of La Notte. *Contemporary Films/McGraw-Hill.*

for the film was also dream-like. Professor Gessner, no doubt fully aware that Fellini considers the colors in a dream to be "concepts, not approximations or memories,"[32] summarized his use of color as follows:

> Throughout the film Fellini uses color as idea. The puritanical and childish past is depicted in pale and sweet tones that remind the viewer of ice-cream flavors. The black, funeral gowns and hoods of the nun-figures are color symbols of repression and death. The hectic and erotic present is shown in riotous reds, fierce purples, glamorous greens, and hot flesh tints.[33]

In the next chapter, we shall have occasion to contrast Fellini's use of color in *Juliet of the Spirits* with that of another distinguished filmmaker, Michelangelo Antonioni.

11

Antonioni and the Plotless Screenplay

Before 1960, the way in which most theatrical films were constructed was directly influenced by the ideas of three very important men: Aristotle, Ibsen and Freud.* Aristotle had indicated in a treatise around 330 B.C. that all plays worthy of the name must contain a plot, which he defined as a series of events connected according to the laws of probability and necessity (or cause and effect); as far as Aristotle was concerned, a playwright (or "play maker," as he termed him) was essentially a maker of plots.† Ibsen, in the late Nineteenth century, introduced a type of play that served as a major model for succeeding playwrights of the next seventy-

---

* Of course, some notable exceptions in films made before 1960 that we have already mentioned are *Diary of a Country Priest, Wild Strawberries,* and *Breathless.*

† More specifically, Aristotle meant that in a properly-constructed plot the events, or incidents, give rise to each other.

five years: drama which takes place in a realistic *milieu* and employs idiomatic dialogue—but more importantly for our purposes, drama in which both the plot and characters are structured, or contrived, so as to prove and/or demonstrate a socially-significant premise. We have already discussed Freud's employment of free association in the psychoanalytic treatment of his (mostly neurotic) patients. However, Freud's greatest influence on drama and film is not limited to any specific technique that he introduced or originated but is to be found in his considerable emphasis on the importance of past events—and especially those of early childhood —as a determinant of present or future behavior.* For Freud, behavior—and especially abnormal behavior—must be explained or analyzed in order to be understood; for this purpose, the *past* most readily holds the key to such an understanding (in film, the flashback remains the most Freudian of all cinematic devices).

The first filmmaker to significantly deviate *and at the same time* signal a major trend away from these aforementioned traditions in cinema was Michelangelo Antonioni, one of motion picture's most extraordinary talents. Antonioni began his film career in Italy in 1939 as the editor of a Fascist cinema magazine (a job that he soon had to give up for political reasons) ; this was then followed by a brief period of study at the Experimental Film Center in Rome. Antonioni's next professional film work consisted of several screenwriting assignments (one of which was in collaboration

---

* More specifically, Freud believed that most neurotic behavior in adults can be traced back to incidents that happen to the individual before the age of six. Most films, however, including those that purport to be actual psycho-analytic case-histories, generally have not gone that far in the use of Freud's theories—i.e. in the emphasis on the importance of *early* childhood events on the development of the personality. Instead, a great many films have dealt with a certain type of neurotic behavior that usually develops from causes that occur *after* early childhood, called *traumatic* neuroses, which is due to excessive fright and severe shock caused by tragic accidents, explosions, etc., and which appears to be easier to cure than neuroses having infantile origins.

with Roberto Rossellini) ; in 1942, he was sent to France by the Italian film company Scalera to work as an assistant director to Marcel Carné on the film *Les Visiteurs du soir*. After finishing work on this picture, Antonioni returned to Rome, where he began work on a documentary on the life of fishermen and river dwellers of the lower Po valley; the subject of this film, *Gente del Po,* consisted of the rudimentary and drab existence of these fishermen and peasants, and indicated a certain sympathy on the part of its director with the aims of neo-realism—shortly to become a dominant trend in Italian cinema (although Antonioni was never to figure very prominently in this movement). After the completion of this film Antonioni wrote articles for film journals, collaborated on several scripts and made more short documentaries. It was not until 1950, at the age of thirty-eight, that Antonioni was to make his first feature film.

Cronaca di un amore

The plot of his first feature, a rather sordid melodrama, is not really important for us; but Antonioni was to face certain problems and make certain discoveries during its production that were to have a profound influence on his future career as a filmmaker. The biggest problem concerned his decision as to what kind of film to make; below, he describes his predicament and how he ultimately solved it:

> I had arrived a little late on the scene, at a time when the first flowering of films [neo-realism], though still valid, was already beginning to show signs of exhaustion. Consequently, I was forced to stop and consider what was the true state of things, what ideas were really being thought. And it seemed to me that perhaps it was no longer so important, as I said before, to examine the relationship between the individual and his environment, as it was to examine the individual himself . . .
>
> And so I began with *Cronaca di un amore,* in which I analyzed the condition of spiritual aridity and a certain type of

moral coldness in the lives of several individuals belonging to the upper middle class strata of Milanese society.[1]

It was this concern of Antonioni, to examine "the individual himself in all his complex and disquieting reality and in his equally complex relations with others,"[2] that led certain French critics to later define his filmmaking style as a kind of "internal neo-realism."

It is important to note also that Antonioni began to develop a technique during the shooting of this picture that was to become one of his most recognizable characteristics— a technique that has much in common with Orson Welles's use of the "sequence-shot," which we have already mentioned. Antonioni describes the birth of this technique as follows:

> My habit of shooting rather long scenes was born spontaneously on the first day of filming *Cronaca di un amore*. Having the camera fixed to its stand immediately caused me real discomfort. I felt paralyzed, as if I were being prevented from following closely the one thing in the film that interested me: I mean, the characters. The next day, I called for a dolly, and I began to follow my characters till I felt the need to move on to another exercise. For me, this was the best way to be real, to be true. Real: inside the scene, exactly as in life. . . . My technique came into being as a function of two things: the camera and the actors.[3]

As has already been mentioned, the plot of *Cronaca di un amore* is rather conventional (the two partners of an adulterous affair plot the murder of the female partner's husband) ; but when the film first opened in Paris in 1951, one critic, Michel Mayoux (writing in *Cahiers du Cinéma*) , was able to discern the direction that Antonioni's career would later take:

> The story [of *Cronaca di un amore*] develops with the rhythm of its own purely internal necessity. In its unfolding, which owes nothing at all to the rules of the drama, it spins no plot; on the contrary, it draws out a discursive tale to which the

word "End" is written only after the play of events has dispersed its three characters.[4]

I vinti (1952), La signora senza camelie (1953) Le amiche (1955) and Il grido (1957)

In his next four feature films following *Cronaca di un amore,* Antonioni continued to make important discoveries and develop new techniques. Earlier in this book we noted that pictorial composition (e.g. the framing of the shot) is primarily employed in film as a means of expressing the feeling, mood and intensity of a subject through the visual elements of color, line, mass and form—almost identical to the way it is employed in painting, photography and theatre. However, in employing composition in his early films, Antonioni went far beyond what had up to then been the accepted conventions. For example, it had long been known in theatre, and subsequently recognized in film, that the position of the actor's body in relation to the audience (e.g. full face and profile) affected the intensity (strong, weak, etc.) of the dialogue delivered by him. Antonioni, on the other hand, discovered that not only was this true but that "a line spoken by an actor in profile doesn't have the same meaning as one given in full-face. Likewise, a phrase addressed to the camera placed above the actor doesn't have the same meaning it would if the camera were placed below him."[5] Thus, pictorial composition in Antonioni's films came to serve as a means of conveying meaning—and sometimes meaning not directly expressed in the script—as well as feeling, intensity and mood. (We shall further explore his use of composition later in this chapter).

As Antonioni became more and more convinced of the necessity "to observe and describe the thoughts and feelings that motivate a man in his march to happiness or death" in his films,[6] he came to believe that it was "much more cine-

matographic* to try to catch a character's thoughts by showing his reactions, whatever they may be, than to wrap the
whole thing up in a speech, than to resort to what practically
amounts to an explanation."[7] The reader may note that Antonioni's approach to depicting the thoughts of a character,
which was described above, differs substantially from the
approach taken by Eisenstein for his proposed adaptation of
Dreiser's *An American Tragedy*, which was described in an
earlier chapter. Eisenstein eschewed the depiction of a character's thoughts by superficial and external manifestations—
e.g. the character's reactions—which Antonioni would seem
to prefer. For Eisenstein, it was necessary to penetrate with
the camera inside the mind of the character; but for Antonioni, who in his first feature films was so coldly objective, it
was absurd to try to penetrate "inside" the mind of a character with his camera: the only thought material available to
the camera (and thus the most cinematic) were the external
manifestations; therefore, the early cinema of Antonioni had
to be a cinema of external reality, consisting of only those
things directly accessible to the camera.

Perhaps the most important discovery about cinema he
made during this early period was concerned with plot and
story construction, the details of which he describes below:

> Thus I have rid myself of much unnecessary technical baggage,
> eliminating all the logical narrative transitions, all those con-
> nective links between sequences where one sequence served as
> the springboard for the one that followed. The reason I did
> this was because it seemed to me—and of this I am firmly con-
> vinced—that cinema today should be tied to truth rather than
> to logic. And the truth of our daily lives is neither mechanical,
> conventional nor artificial, as stories generally are, and if films
> are made that way, they will show it. The rhythm of life is not
> made up of one steady beat; it is, instead, a rhythm that is

---

* *Cinematographic* is a word derived from the French and Italian words
and means almost the same thing as *cinematic,* but more strongly implies
the meanings "that which is peculiar to cinema," and/or "that which cinema
can do best."

sometimes fast, sometimes slow; it remains motionless for a while, then at the next moment it starts spinning around. There are times when it appears almost static, there are other times when it moves with tremendous speed, and I believe all this should go into the making of a film. I'm not saying one should slavishly follow the day-to-day routine of life, but I think that through these pauses, through this attempt to adhere to a definite reality—spiritual, internal, and even moral— there springs forth what today is more and more coming to be known as modern cinema, that is, a cinema which is not so much concerned with externals as it is with those forces that move us to act in a certain way and not in another. Because the important thing is this: that our acts, our words are nothing more than the consequences of our own personal situation in relation to the world around us.[8]

A cinema "tied to truth rather than to logic," structured according to the "rhythm of life" (although not "slavishly"), and not according to dramatic conventions—that was what would come to be known as "The Cinema of Antonioni."

L'avventura

It was not until 1960, when his sixth feature film was shown at the Cannes Film Festival, that Antonioni's cinematic techniques and discoveries were to achieve the worldwide recognition and attention they so rightly deserved (up until that time, Antonioni was little known outside his own country, and none of his previous five features had yet been released in the United States). The following is his own summary of the plot of this extraordinary film, which descended upon the international film scene like a bombshell:

> Superficially, *L'avventura* may seem to be a love story, perhaps a somewhat mysterious one. During an excursion, a girl disappears. This fact creates a void which is immediately filled by other facts. For the fiancé and for one of the girl's friends, the search for her becomes a kind of sentimental journey at the end of which they both find themselves in a new and quite unforseen situation.[9]

What infuriated many of those who first saw *L'avventura* at Cannes was that they never did find out what became of the girl (Anna) who disappears—whether she is alive or dead—making the film, as Antonioni himself pointed out, a kind of "a mystery film in reverse."[10] This is not as illogical as it may seem, as Pierre Leprohon observes:

> According to age-old dramatic concepts, a story is constructed on a so-called logical foundation and centered on a logical sequence of events. In this light, *L'avventura* is an illogical film. But what concerns Antonioni—and he has repeated this point often—is the characters and their relation to themselves and to events. Why, then, should he sustain interest in facts that have ceased to interest the heroes of the story he is telling? The search for Anna, the court inquest, the consultation and interrogation of witnesses, are meaningful as long as they pre-occupy the principal characters. When new facts take their place in the characters' minds, when new feelings are aroused, the earlier ones crumble away, lose all the reason they ever had for being dwelt upon.[11]

This was indeed a revolutionary concept in 1960: for an author to concern himself with only those things that interest his characters—and not his audience—was akin to giving them a life of their own, something utterly unheard of in cinema at that time. For did Aristotle not teach us that characters along with the plot must obey the law of probability and necessity? And Ibsen, that characters must be manipulated and contrived so as to prove a premise? No wonder that *L'avventura* created such a stir: over two thousand years of theatrical tradition had crumbled before the eyes of those who first saw this quite remarkable film at the Cannes festival in 1960.

La notte (*1961*)

While *L'avventura* did deviate significantly from previous theatrical traditions, it still contained one age-old dramatic element—although perhaps unintentionally—suspense. In Antonioni's next film, however, even this element is lacking: we are not so much concerned with whether or not the protagonists find a way out of their predicament, but with the magnitude of their problem and how they go about solving it (or perhaps their lack of concern about finding a solution).

La notte ("The Night") examines an intellectual crisis that is faced by an Italian writer, Giovanni; his relationship with his wife, Lidia; and the disintegration of his marriage—all three of which are obviously inter-related. An American film of the same period and with much the same subject matter would probably have concentrated on the reasons for the writer's mental state and the failure of his marriage—*à la* Freud—relying heavily on the use of flashbacks. However, Antonioni does no such thing: he does not attempt to analyze the situation—there are no flashbacks; he merely presents the situation as it exists for our examination, which covers approximately eighteen hours in the life of the protagonists. This one day (and night) in the life of the protagonists is not, however, just any ordinary day; in fact, it is a very important day, when a great deal of self-knowledge is to be gained (the couple come to the terrible realization that they no longer love each other), but encased within the rhythm of everyday life, which, as we have seen, so often serves as the internal logic and structure of Antonioni's films. Ostensibly it would seem that the film has no plot, but as Pierre Leprohon points out, the film itself is "the climax of a long, slowly-developed plot, which, day by day, year by year, has led its protagonists closer to their moment of self-awareness."[12]

While having all the makings of a masterpiece, *La notte* is marred by a few serious errors; one of the most serious of which is Antonioni's concentration on the *wrong* character. This was not the first time that Antonioni had made such a mistake; in *L'avventura* he concentrated too much on Sandro (played by Gabriele Ferzetti), the philandering and spiritually sterile architect, instead of the insecure and complex Claudia (played by Monica Vitti). In *La notte*, the error was to concentrate too heavily on Giovanni (played by Marcello Mastroianni), the writer in crisis, who closely resembles the Sandro of *L'avventura* in his erotic infidelity, instead of developing more fully the enigmatic character of the wife, Lidia (played by Jeanne Moreau). Why are these "mistakes"? Because the reality that is filtered through his "intellectual" characters*—and always men in Antonioni's films—is superficial and empty, and the so-called crises that they undergo are often more pretentious than serious: e.g. Giovanni says in *La notte*, "The way I feel right now, I don't know how I'll ever be able to write again. It's not that I don't know what to write, but how to write it. That's what they call a 'crisis'."[14] It is not, then, the intellectual types in both *L'avventura* and *La notte* that are the most striking characters, but the women in the two films; on this subject Antonioni has said: "I always give a great deal of importance to the feminine characters because I believe that I know women better than I do men. I think that reality can be filtered better through women's psychologies. They are more instinctive, more sincere."[15] To summarize: it is not the men in Antonioni's films who provide the most effective means of filtering reality, but the women—who allow themselves to be guided more by instinct than by intellect.

Another serious flaw in *La notte* is in the film's ending. Although, as we have previously quoted him, Antonioni finds it more cinematic to visually express a character's thoughts

---

* In discussing his preference for intellectual characters, Antonioni has said that he chooses them for his films

mainly because they have a greater awareness of what is happening to them, and also because they have a more refined sensibility, a more subtle sense of intuition through which I can filter the kind of reality I am interested in expressing, whether it be an internal reality or an external one. Furthermore, the intellectual, more than others, is the type of person in which I can find the symptoms of that particular kind of crisis which I am interested in describing.[13]

"rather than by wrapping the whole thing up in a speech, an explanation," he apparently disregarded his own insight by concluding *La notte* with a long conversation between the writer and his wife; the following is an excerpt from that conversation (spoken by Lidia, the wife) :

> The reason I feel like dying tonight is because I don't love you any more. (*Moving nervously*) That's why I feel so miserable. I wish I were already old and that my entire life had already been dedicated to you. I wish I didn't exist any more, because I can no longer love you. There it is. That's the thought that came to me when we were sitting in that night-club and you were so bored.[16]

Antonioni explains that this conversation is "really a soliloquy, a monologue by the wife, a kind of summing-up of the film to clarify the real meaning of what took place."[17] Needless to say, this "summing-up"—which can perhaps be partly justified by the fact that at this particular moment in the film the wife simply wanted to *verbalize* her problem—is the weakest part of the entire script.

Now that we have dealt with some of the deficiencies of *La notte*, let us proceed to examine some of its strengths, of which there are many.

Antonioni is able to raise *La notte* to the level of the exceptional and the extraordinary not only by his almost total elimination of traditional dramatic structure and devices, along with his uncompromising adherence to the natural rhythms of life, but also by his use of both outward manifestations and actions (along with visual images) to reveal the thoughts of his characters (or at least one of them, the wife). His preference for the latter two techniques—outward manifestations and actions—of revealing character-thought is evident throughout not only the film but the entire screenplay as well: the script is practically devoid of any description of the characters' states of mind; the following excerpt, taken from the beginning of the screenplay, which describes a very emotionally-charged moment for the writer's wife, illustrates this point:

> Lidia steps out of the doorway of the hospital and walks hurriedly to the car. She sits down, visibly shaken, on the front seat. She searches around in her purse for cigarettes, takes one out of the pack, and puts it into her mouth. But she flings it away and bursts into a fit of uncontrollable weeping.[18]

Note that in the excerpt above we are never told why Lidia is weeping, nor is there any dialogue or off-screen voice to tell us what she is thinking; everything is expressed, instead, through her outward manifestations and actions.

There is one very famous sequence in *La notte* that best exemplifies Antonioni's use of external action, and therefore deserves our closest attention: Lidia's wanderings through the city and suburbs of Milan (the setting for the film). This sequence occurs just after the writer's wife has left a party given for her husband by his publisher; the following, an excerpt from the screenplay, describes her walk:

> She starts walking slowly and aimlessly along the street, ignoring and ignored by the thick crowds. . . . On a deserted, sunlit street, Lidia strolls along looking at the modern apartment and office buildings. They appear cold and faceless. Lidia feels completely alienated from the surroundings. It is very hot. . . .
> Lidia walks on and reaches a spot where there is an open space between the tall, glass-covered buildings. The sun beats down on the narrow space. She looks at the patch of sky above the buildings as though longing to flee these oppressive walls. Suddenly, a low-flying jet thunders overhead, filling the streets and the open space with a sinister roar. Lidia hurries away as though terrified. Running to a tree-lined street, she looks behind her as though someone were following her. She feels calmer and wanders on slowly. She picks up a leaf and examines it.[19]

"How are we to regard Lidia's interminable wanderings, first through the chaos of urban life, then through the apparent tranquility of the suburb, if not as a long continuous interior monologue, as the kaleidoscopic image of a disintegrating world that looms up within herself?" has remarked critic Guido Aristarco.[20] And indeed, that is just what they are: a stream of consciousness expressed exclusively through external manifestations and actions—and never verbalized, even in the script. Certainly this is a very far cry from the stream of consciousness cinematic technique outlined by Eisenstein. What counts the most, however, is the effectiveness of Antonioni's technique: we are able to get inside the mind of the character in a manner that is most inobtrusive, and not at all awkward.

Among the most notable aspects of *La notte* is its imaginative employment of visual images; however, in order to understand just how Antonioni creatively uses images in this film, we must first learn how images are employed in motion pictures in general.

Visual Images

There are three main types of visual images generally employed in film, although any single image may sometimes have the characteristics of more than one type. The first and most frequently employed can be best understood as an example of "picturization," which, we previously learned, is essentially a visual *representation* of a narrative action. A second, but infrequently-used image is the "symbol," which *stands* for an idea or concept but does not represent it; in *Juliet of the Spirits*, the image of the Christian martyr being burned on the grating is such an example. Of much greater interest to us, however, is the third type of image, which makes extensive use of compositional principles. This third category can be sub-divided into those images which generally utilize composition to express mood or feeling and those which use composition primarily for the purpose of conveying meaning—i.e. the relationship between persons, or persons

and things—and sometimes, as in *La notte,* even thought.*
It is the latter sub-division, i.e. those images that are composed in such a way as to show the relationship between
different things or between things and abstract concepts and/
or ideas, that most resemble verbal images such as metaphors
and similes; and just as we may judge a writer by the quality
of his verbal images, we may also evaluate a filmmaker in
the same way—by the quality of his visual images.

Certainly, when the quality of his own images are discussed, Antonioni has no need to be modest or ashamed: "I
have always tried to fill the image with a greater suggestive-
ness," he has said,[21] and certainly his films would bear this
out with their abundance of images that have a rare expressiveness. One of the best examples of this is in *La notte,*
during the stream of consciousness wanderings through Milan by the writer's wife—a long shot, from an extremely high
angle, which shows Lidia completely dwarfed by the wall
of a tall skyscraper. The script says that the buildings in this
shot appear "cold and faceless," and that "Lidia feels completely alienated from the surroundings";[22] the script *tells*
us this, however, while Antonioni's visual image more per-

---

* Rudolf Arnheim, on page 137 of his book *Visual Thinking* (Berkeley and
Los Angeles, University of California Press, 1969), presents a brilliant discussion of the subject of visual images as they primarily apply to painting,
which is not very different from their application to film. Arnheim uses
"abstractness"—which he defines as the means by which a picture interprets
what it portrays—as the fundamental quality for distinguishing and classi-
fying the various types of images. Since the first type described above seeks
not to *interpret* what it portrays but only to *represent* it, it would therefore
be considered to be at a very low level of abstractness—if it possesses that
quality at all. The second category of images, the symbols, are designated
as such, according to Arnheim, because they portray "things which are at a
higher level of abstractness than is the symbol itself." The last category of
images, those that Arnheim calls "pictures," are classified as such only "to
the extent to which they portray things located at a lower level of abstractness than they are themselves." Arnheim then goes on to say that
images such as these "do their work by grasping and rendering some relevant qualities—shape, color, movement—of the objects or activities they
depict."

fectly *expresses* it. This image indicates a very important tendency in Antonioni's works: their concentration on inanimate objects. "I have a great sympathy with things, perhaps even more than with people, though it is the latter that interest me more," he has said,[23] although this statement only partly explains this particular aspect of his work; for Antonioni is not only interested in studying the relationships between people but also those between individuals and their surroundings.

L'eclisse (*1962*)

In his next feature film, Antonioni continued to expand and perfect the techniques noted in *La notte* and *L'avventura*. *L'eclisse* ("The Eclipse") is the third and final part of the trilogy examining the phenomenon of love (or lack of it) in our time—a modern love story (*ca.* 1962). From the way Antonioni himself has described this film as a story "about a young working woman who leaves a man because she no longer loves him, and then leaves another man because she still loves him," and the way in which the actress (Monica Vitti) who plays the heroine has described it—it is, she has said, "the story of a love that lasts for a short time —as brief as an eclipse," adding that she refused with all her being "to accept the truth that she [the heroine] accepts: the fragility of relationships and their inevitable end"[24]—one would indeed surmise that it is a tragedy, totally saturated with feelings and emotions of anxiety, desperation and despair. Yet this is a very deceptive view: throughout much of *L'eclisse* the mood is light-hearted and gay, mainly because in this new love affair both partners readily accept the temporary nature of their relationship and therefore do not expect too much from it.

Although plot is reduced to a minimum in *L'eclisse*, it is probably Antonioni's most studied and precise screenplay; yet, on the other hand, it is probably his most contrived

scripting endeavor—with entrances, exits and meetings between characters frequently being embarrassingly awkward.
The film (apparently avoided the mistakes of *L'avventura*
and *La notte*) deals primarily with one character, a young
working woman, Vittoria (played by Monica Vitti), and her
troubled love life, beginning with her termination of an
unsuccessful affair with a man much older than herself (and
in typical Antonioni style we are given very few details about
this affair or the reasons for its failure) and endng with the
establishment of a new relationship with a younger man,
Piero (played by Alain Delon)—with a very strong implication throughout that this new affair will be very short-lived.

Something new for Antonioni, this film contains a very
unusual interior documentary on the Roman stock exchange
(Vittoria's new lover is a stockbroker) and an Eisensteinian
montage at the end that in an abstract manner attempts to
tie together all the narrative and thematic threads of the film
into one unified statement. Of the two elements just mentioned, the interior documentary on the stock exchange,
though expertly done, is integrated into the film the most
poorly. Ostensibly this digression into the world of money
and banking would appear to illustrate the prison of invest-
ments and speculations that Vittoria's new lover, Piero, is
trapped in, and which affects his every aspect, including his
love life; but Antonioni's premise—that the "world today is
ruled by money, greed for money, fear of money" and that
this "leads to a dangerous passivity towards problems of the
spirit"[25]—seems to become lost in this story where the two
protagonists are so vibrantly alive, much more alive than the
so-called intellectual types of his two earlier films who spend
most of their time commiserating about their spiritual vacu-
ity. The second unusual element in *L'eclisse*—for Antonioni
—is the *montage* at the end, which is far more successful; in
it Antonioni juxtaposes several shots (fifty-eight in all) which
show the places—in the modern EUR section of Rome—
where most of the liaisons between Vittoria and Piero took

place and where they were, for brief moments, so happy; but shots in which the two lovers are conspicuously absent, perhaps a comment on the permanence of things and objects contrasted with the ephemeral nature of human relationships.

Stanley Kauffman found in *L'eclisse,* in the characterization of the heroine, what he thought to be a deficiency; he wrote that in actuality "Vittoria is more a symbol than a person—almost a pageant figure, the Spirit of the Modern Girl. Her uncertainties and frustrations seem selected to represent a social group, rather than to create *her.*"[26] Indeed, this is true: Vittoria is a symbol, and when she says to her new lover, "I wish I didn't love you . . . Or that I loved you much more,"[27] she is not speaking of only her dilemma but the dilemma of newly-emancipated and -liberated women all over the world. Yet in spite of all her "uncertainties and frustrations," Vittoria *is* able to love, to enjoy brief moments of happiness, to live. Thanks to Monica Vitti's engaging performance, the character of Vittoria is given both substance and texture; this so-called Spirit of the Modern Girl no longer is a symbol but a real person instead—and a vibrantly alive one at that.

Up to this point we have paid very little attention to the subject matter of Antonioni's films: the sterility in the lives of certain middle class—and even upper class—people, and the alienation and lack of communication and love between them. This neglect has been intentional; for the *nature* of Antonioni's reality is not as important in the development of film as an art as the *approach* he has used in describing it. But there is one important aspect of Antonioni's films connected with their subject matter that we should perhaps mention, and that is that for the most part they appear to present problems but never any solutions. We have previously made the same observation about neo-realist films; but whereas Zavattini defended neo-realism by saying that it was really only necessary to present problems, Antonioni frankly admits that he has no solutions. "Inasmuch as I am the product of a middle class society, and am preoccupied with making middle class dramas, I am not equipped to do so," he has said. "The middle class doesn't give me the means with which to resolve any middle class problems. That's why I confine myself to pointing out existing problems without proposing any solutions. I think it is equally important to point them out as it is to propose solutions."[28]

Deserto rosso (1964)

Of all Antonioni's films this is unquestionably his most masterful—the culmination and complete perfection of his previous cinematic techniques and discoveries, as well as his first experiment in the use of color. We have to go back to Antonioni's segment for Zavattini's *Love in the City* in 1954, a very dry and objective examination of people who had actually attempted suicide, to find him taking such a clinical approach toward his subject matter, which in this case is the mental deterioration of a young, married woman (again played by Monica Vitti). All of the characteristic Antonioni techniques are in evidence here (e.g. minimal plot, expressive and meaningful images, and outward manifestation of thought); however, he has added a new technique in *Deserto rosso* (*The Red Desert*) —*color*, which besides making the film extraordinarily beautiful, greatly increases its expressiveness.

Antonioni's use of color, a completely subjective use, signals a departure from one of his more characteristic approaches—the depiction of character thought through external manifestations—since in this film, for the first time, he attempts to penetrate with his camera directly into the minds of his protagonists. Images go in and out of focus—coinciding with the heroine's disturbed mental states—and the colors that we see are by and large exactly those that the characters see (Antonioni is reported to have painted a marsh gray for this film because that was the way his characters felt when they looked at it). The importance of color in *Deserto rosso* is clearly indicated in both the screenplay and dialogue. For example, when the distraught heroine, Giuliana, goes to the hotel room of a friend of her husband's, the man (Corrado) asks her what it is she wants protection from; she replies, "From the streets, from the factories, from the *colors,* from the sky, from people!"[29] (The story takes place in the modern port city of Ravenna, Italy, the colors of which—brilliant reds and oranges and yellows—has for Antonioni a certain "industrial *ambiance.*") Earlier in this same scene, the script describes Giuliana, who is tidying up the hotel room of Corrado, in the following manner—again with a great deal of emphasis on color:

> *GIULIANA removes her overcoat and begins to pick up a jacket, a tie, some handkerchiefs, a shirt, some colored envelopes, and place them on the bureau or on chairs, not following a logical order but according to her own system: all the green objects together, all the red together, all the yellow, etc.*

Soon afterwards Giuliana and Corrado make love, and the ending to this scene is described in the screenplay as follows:

> *Some time later, GIULIANA and CORRADO are in the bed, completely naked, motionless, immersed in an unreal pink light. The entire room is pink: the objects, the furniture, the clothing.*[31]

We have seen how Fellini used color in *Juliet of the Spirits*—symbolically—to express ideas; on the other hand, Antonioni uses color in *Deserto rosso—metaphorically—*to express thoughts and feelings (e.g. "Everything seemed gray"), and in this case the thoughts and feelings of a severely psychologically-disturbed young woman.

Antonioni's use of color in *Deserto rosso,* along with his highly-expressive images, brings up a point that may have been only hinted at previously in this book: the possibility of there being, and expressing, *non-verbal thought,* i.e. thought that does not first appear in our minds in the form of words, and is therefore inadequately expressed by them—thoughts that are more associated with color, composition and mood than with syntax or logic. If such a mental phenomenon does exist, then Antonioni is its most eloquent practitioner—and *Deserto rosso* its most masterful demonstration.

Antonioni As a Director

The directorial approach of Antonioni, perhaps more than that of any other filmmaker with whom we have dealt, best exemplifies the basic premise of this book: that filmmaking is one continuous creative process from the first stage of the writing or scripting right through to completion.

How is a film born in Antonioni? Here is his answer: "A picture probably has its birth in the disorder within us, and that's the difficulty: putting things in order. Knowing how to pick out the right thread from the skein."[32] Thus, the most critical talent for a director to possess at that early stage, according to Antonioni, is the ability "to recognize an idea out of the chaos of feelings, reflections, observations, impulses which the surrounding world stirs up in us."[33] For Antonioni it is these beginning stages of a film's creation, i.e. the writing stages, which are also the most arduous and frustrating; this is perhaps not at all surprising for a man who is more at home with visual images than with words. "You have to describe images with provisional words which later will no longer have any use," he has bemoaned about writing scripts. And what is even more unnatural, "You sometimes end up describing weather conditions," he has added, offering the following as an example: "The sky is clear, but large clouds block the horizon. As though coming out of these clouds, X's car appears on the horizon."[34] All these things have thus led Antonioni to conclude, "Screenplays are on the way to becoming actually sheets of notes for those who, at the camera, will write the film themselves."[35]

However, it is not Antonioni's ideas on screenplay writing (which are not too different from other filmmakers whom we have dealt with) that makes him almost unique, but his approach to filmmaking once he has arrived on the set. Here, Antonioni believes, "The best results are obtained by the 'collision' that takes place between the environment in which the scene is to be shot and my own particular state of mind at the specific moment"; or, in other words, he believes that the "most direct way to recreate a scene is to enter into a *rapport* with the environment itself."[36] It is for this reason that Antonioni is wary of very detailed planning beforehand, especially where the shots are concerned: "Obviously, in the various stages of preparing a film, a director creates images in his mind," he has pointed out, "but it is always dangerous to fall in love with these formulated images, because you eventually end up by running after images abstracted from the reality of the environment in which the scene is being shot and which are no longer the same as they first appeared while sitting behind the desk."[37]

12

The Underground Cinema

We have already had occasion to mention two very important movements in the recent history of film, neo-realism and the New Wave (although the latter has been mentioned only incidentally), both of which arose from an extreme dissatisfaction with, if not an outright abhorrence of, the commercial cinema in their countries of origin. However, no matter how much the proponents of neo-realism, and, several years later, the New Wave decried commercial cinema, their own films were nevertheless commercially-oriented in respect to both the professional backgrounds and artistic goals of those who made them and the way in which they were financed and distributed. Practically all of the neo-realist directors and scriptwriters had worked extensively in the pre-war commercial (and Fascist) film industry in Italy; the New Wave, while generally only connected with the outer fringes of French commercial film production in its beginning, had as its most cherished dream, according to Jean-Luc Godard, "to shoot *Spartacus* in Hollywood with ten million dollars."[1] In contrast, the American Underground filmmakers, whom we shall now examine, launched a prolific, if not extraordinarily productive, movement in cinema that while also critical of the commercial cinema in its own country (and specifically Hollywood cinema), possessed none of the above-mentioned characteristics: commercial orientation and/or professional experience on the part of its practitioners.

The American Underground cinema was and still is a loosely-knit group of independent filmmakers from quite diversified backgrounds whose main bond appears to be their uniform lack of access to the regular channels of commercial film production and distribution in America (however, as we shall later see, this particular criterion may be changing). Included in this large group of filmmakers are some extremely talented makers of abstract films, who live, or once lived, for the most part in California, such as Jordan Belson, John and James Whitney, Harry Smith and Bruce Baillie. However, the most influential and best-known segment of the Underground film movement grew out of what has sometimes been called the New York "school," which consisted of several people who had, during the late Forties and Fifties, specialized in the making of low budget, semi-professional films that primarily dealt with contemporary social problems; the better-known filmmakers from this school include Sidney Myers, Lionel Rogosin, Alfred Leslie, Robert Frank, Shirley Clark, John Cassavetes, Ricky Leacock, Morris Engel and Don Pennebaker (the last three particularly noted for their introduction of new, lightweight portable equipment which has greatly facilitated motion-picture production, both documentary and feature). Also working in New York at about the same time but not really aesthetically related to them, were Stan Vanderbeek, best known for his numerous social and political protest films, satirical in nature, which make extensive use of both animation and collage, and Stan Brakhage, whose films are perhaps as poetic and lyrical as they are crude and styleless; the work of these two filmmakers was also to have a profound influence on the emerging Underground film movement in America.

In September of 1960, several American independent filmmakers (mostly from the New York school) met together to discuss their common interests—which led to the formation of the New American Cinema Group. Besides having the urgent need to establish an alternate means for both producing and distributing their own films outside of normal commercial channels, this very disparate group of filmmakers were united by another common but equally important bond: their utter contempt and complete disdain for Hollywood and all the values, both cinematic and social, that they believed it then stood for (and possibly still does). In fact, the first statement issued by the New American Cinema Group included the following rather scathing denunciation of Hollywood films (and all so-called official cinema wherever it might exist in the world) along with a not too subtle indication of the direction in which the Group itself would go:

> The very slickness of their execution [of the "official cinema," that is] has become a perversion covering the falsity of their themes, their lack of sensitivity, their lack of style. . . .
> We don't want false, polished, slick films—we prefer them rough, unpolished, but alive; we don't want rosy films—we want them the color of blood.[2]

It would be a mistake, however, if we were to consider the New American Cinema as something separate and distinct from related activity in the other arts in America at about the same time. In fact, the New American Cinema was very much influenced by, if not a direct outgrowth of, the "Beats," or "Beat Generation," a small but influential group of poets and writers who frequented the bohemian coffee houses in both New York and San Francisco during the mid- and late Fifties and who were the first literary group in America to raise a critical murmur during the Eisenhower ("Peace and Prosperity") years, expressing their views with much unbridled sexuality and utter disregard for traditional American values.* Needless to say, the New American Cinema wholeheartedly adopted the Beat's disquieting vision of America as their own—a vision in which they saw Hollywood as its most perverse reflection.

Interestingly enough, the most prolific filmmakers (and best known) of the New American Cinema are those who are primarily associated with what can best be described as a "Cinema of the Absurd," and about whom Jonas Mekas has written: "With their own lives they create a 'cinema reality' that is tense to the point of explosion. In a sense, they don't have to 'invent': they just have to turn the camera upon themselves, or upon their close friends, and it explodes into the pyrotechniques upon which no imagination could improve."[3] Probably the best example of a filmmaker whose work embodies the philosophy and techniques of this Cinema of the Absurd is the late Ron Rice, who allegedly invented the whole *genre* back in 1960, when he made his now famous Underground classic *The Flower Thief;* the following is Rice's own description of the origin of his quite remarkable film:

> In the old Hollywood days movie studios would keep a man on the set who, when all other sources of ideas failed (writers, directors), was called upon to "cook up" something for filming. He was called the Wild Man. *The Flower Thief* has been put together in memory of all dead wild men who died unnoticed in the field of stunt.[4]

There is just one word that will adequately describe *The Flower Thief*—wild. Loosely about the wanderings of its Beatnik, non-actor "star," Taylor Mead, the film combines

---

* It is worthwhile noting that one of the most famous films to come out of the New York school was Alfred Leslie and Robert Frank's *Pull My Daisy* (1958), which was based on a play, *The Beat Generation,* by "Beat" writer Jack Kerouac, who actually spoke the film's narration.

excerpts from Beat poetry readings, lectures on LSD and penology, libidinous hetero- and homosexuality and slapstick comedy into a raw masterpiece, which is technically characterized by very crude editing and under-exposed and outdated filmstock. However, if *The Flower Thief* was "wild," then Jack Smith's *Flaming Creatures* (1963), another example of this Cinema of the Absurd, would have to be called "indescribable"; "Film Culture," in awarding it their Fifth Independent Film Award, remarked that Smith's film (essentially nothing more than a transvestite orgy) struck them "with not the mere pity or curiosity of the perverse, but the glory, the pageantry of Transylvestia and the magic of Fairyland."[5] Unfortunately, *Flaming Creatures* has remained more talked about than seen, for it was confiscated by local police shortly after its first public showing (in New York City). By 1963–64 the tone of the Cinema of the Absurd, and to a certain extent the entire New York Underground, had become fairly uniform: rather amateurish, technically inept films (like home movies) made with mostly amateur equipment and usually employing exhibitionistic non-actors—and, for the most part, having a definite homosexual orientation.

One rather interesting characteristic of the Cinema of the Absurd was its pre-occupation with Hollywood—to many Underground filmmakers nothing more than a homosexual put-on. Ronald Tavel, a playwright closely associated with the Theatre of the Ridiculous in New York and author of numerous scenarios for Underground films, gives an explanation for this pre-occupation:

> Hollywood is the mythology that Americans have in common. It is not an exaggeration to claim that the historical product of Hollywood functions very much as the Greek myths for old Greece. Hollywood embodies the ambitions and daydreams of the American populace and, more importantly, its peculiar interpretations of the complex cosmos surrounding it. . . .
> Hollywood, then, is the background and material for the art of the New American Cinema, much as Greek mythology was the subject matter-at-hand for the art of Homer and Sophocles.[6]

What did Tavel think of such famous Hollywood stars as Jean Harlow and Marilyn Monroe?

> Jean Harlow is a transvestite, as are Mae West and Marilyn Monroe, in the same sense that their feminineness is so exaggerated that it becomes a commentary on womanhood rather than the real thing or representation of realness.[7]

How faithful was the Underground or New American Cinema to the Hollywood myth?

> It [the New American Cinema] has a way of holding faith with Hollywood for all its savageness . . . in order to insist on its [Hollywood's] promise and perhaps foster its fulfillment. That the promise is the sham and its product sheer horror seems not to mitigate the naivete of the New American Cinema.[8]

And, in fact, the Underground itself soon became nothing more than a microcosm of Hollywood, with the creation of its own "stars" and "superstars," and accompanied by all the vanity and viciousness that fills movie gossip columns throughout the world; as a result Tavel himself gave up working in the New American Cinema because he could no longer stomach the "Frankenstein" that he had helped create.

However, not everyone connected with the Underground was as contemptuous of Hollywood as Ronald Tavel: Jack Smith, for example, claimed that Maria Montez (a film star in the Forties of low-budget, exotic Hollywood films, who even Smith admits was the World's Worst Actress) was his favorite movie star;* and up in the Bronx (New York City), Mike and George Kuchar began their Underground careers by making 8mm films with titles such as *I Was a Teen Age Rumpot* (1960), *Born of the Wind* (1961) and *Lust for Ecstasy* (1963), which, although they were parodies of Holly-

---

* Smith is alleged to have "discovered" for his *Flaming Creatures* a female impersonator who has since patterned himself after the late Miss Montez—even to the extent of adopting the screen name of Mario Montez (in *Flaming Creatures*, however, he uses the name Dolores Flores) —and who became an important "star" of Underground films.

wood films, were at least affectionate parodies, made with people that were, according to Mike Kuchar, "fat, but they wanted to be Marilyn Monroe."[9]

Andy Warhol

Among all the filmmakers associated with the Absurdist element of the New American Cinema Andy Warhol has become the most prominent; in fact, to the majority of the general public—filmgoing or not—Warhol's name is the first, if not only one, that they associate with the whole Underground film movement in America. Already a successful Pop artist before venturing on the Underground scene, Warhol was a Johnny-come-lately to the New American Cinema, not making his first film until 1963, the year in which he is reported to have acquired his first movie camera. Warhol soon became, nevertheless, one of the most prolific filmmakers of the entire movement; so prolific, in fact, that just four years after Warhol made his first film, critic Sheldon Renan was able to divide this extraordinary filmmaker's work into roughly four periods (although Renan is quick to point out that Warhol's combined films actually constitute "part of one huge work, the definitive documentary on the socialites, starlets, addicts, homosexuals, fashion models, artists and people-on-the-make who comprise New York's bizarre demi-monde"[10]).

The films of Warhol's first period (for this discussion, we shall use Renan's divisions), such as *Eat* (1963), *Sleep* (1963), *Haircut* (1964), *Kiss* (1964), and *Empire* (1964), were primarily characterized by their static photography (e.g. little or no camera movement) and very mundane subjects (e.g. a man sleeping for six hours and the Empire State Building photographed uninterruptedly from dawn to dusk). It is not at all surprising, given the unorthodox length of these first films (along with the fact that little or nothing happened in them), that the preponderance of critical opinion concerning Andy Warhol as a novice filmmaker was that he was either a charlatan or a fraud, or at best the perpetrator of a bizarre put-on, meant as an insult to the intelligence of his audience (many of whom had paid two or three dollars to see these marathon films) .* Yet nothing could have been further from the truth, for what Warhol was attempting to do was to discover the artistic potentialities inherent in the film medium, as if he himself were the first filmmaker ever to conduct such an inquiry.† In this regard, critic Gregory Battcock sees a film such as Warhol's *Empire* as not a mere put-on, but as "an investigation of the presence and character of film . . . And the terms established for this investigation are the black-and-white film technology and the obvious yet frequently-denied limitation of time [by 'time' Battcock means that the filmmaker (Warhol) decides how long the film will run—in this case eight hours—and not the au-

---

* Not all of the critical opinion about Warhol was unfavorable, however. To many New Yorkers, the early films of the former Pop artist were *high camp*—which we shall discuss later—and very *in*. Gerard Malanga, himself a former star of Warhol films, writes the following about Baby Jane Holzer, an early Warhol "starlet" who achieved instant fame within New York's "in" set:

> It was her diminutive charm and her natural effervescence which prevented her from remaining long in the background at a time when the "underground" patrons were calling for pop, punch, and passion. Soon she broke into greater prominence in such pictures as Andy Warhol's *Couch* and *Kiss*. So realistic was her go-go-yeah-yeahing in the last two films that Jane was promoted to stardom by the New York press, *Show* magazine art director Nicky Haslam, high fashion photographers David Bailey and Jerry Schatzberg, and American *Vogue* editor-in-chief Diana Vreeland, and made a series of three-minute portrait studies for Andy Warhol in *13 Most Beautiful Women*, which led Tom Wolfe to write a long conversational piece called "The Girl of the Year" which appeared in *The Sunday Herald Tribune's* magazine section *New York*.11

†Warhol was probably not jesting when he said (in an interview in 1966) that the filmmaker that has influenced him the most is Thomas Edison, who can probably be considered the world's first film-maker, and whose first works, like Warhol's, were also very static.12 Compare this with Jean-Luc Godard's stated purpose in making his first film, *Breathless:* "What I wanted to do was . . . remake, but differently, everything that had already been done in the cinema. I wanted to give the impression of just finding or experiencing the process of cinema for the first time."13

dience]."[14] Battcock further explains this by pointing out that "the selection of the Empire State Building is primarily a device through which to present the full range of tones from black to white, the first reel of the long movie pictures the dramatic change of all the original darks or blacks to lights, and the original lights gradually moving through the entire spectrum, to blacks."[15]

Film Culture—in awarding him their Sixth Independent Film Award (1964)—also noted the experimental and exploratory nature of Warhol's first period films:

> Andy Warhol is taking cinema back to its origins, to the days of Lumière, for a rejuvenation and a cleansing. . . . With his artist's intuition as his only guide, he records, almost obsessively, man's daily activities, the things he sees around him.
> The first thing he does is that he stops us from running. His camera rarely moves. It stays fixed on the subject like there was nothing more beautiful and no thing more important than that subject. It stays there longer than we are used to. Long enough for us to begin to free ourselves from all that we thought about haircutting or eating or the Empire State Building; or, for that matter, about cinema. We begin to realize that we have never, really, seen haircutting, or eating. We have cut our hair, we have eaten, but we have never really seen those actions. The whole reality around us becomes *differently* interesting, and we feel like we have to begin filming everything anew. A new way of looking at things and at the screen is given through the personal vision of Warhol . . .[16]

If it can be accurately said that the films of Warhol's first period explored the potentialities of black-and-white cinematography, then the films of his second period, his first to use sound, should be characterized as explorations of the potentialities of the sound film—and, just as was the case with the first sound films made in Hollywood in the late Twenties, Warhol's first experiments with sound were also "one hundred per cent talkies," with the actors (or "non-actors") in these films constantly engaging in incessant chatter. Primarily scripted by Ronald Tavel, these second period Warhol films were essentially vicious parodies of the Hollywood myth, which, more often than not, "starred" female impersonator Mario Montez. A typical film of this period is *Harlot* (1965), which is a fictionalization of the movie career of Jean Harlow (portrayed here by Mario Montez). A brief synopsis of the film's action is as follows: four non-actors are statically photographed as they stare blankly at the camera, during which time one of them eats five bananas, two exchange cigarettes and another pours a glass of water over someone's head; all this while the film's "raunchy" commentary is being provided by three off-screen persons (one of whom was Ronald Tavel) reading, often inaudibly, into a microphone.

Warhol's third period is comprised of films primarily scripted by Chuck Wein; the best-known film from this period is *My Hustler* (1965), essentially a semi-documentary on male, homosexual prostitutes. *My Hustler,* along with several other films that belong to Warhol's third period, is characterized by a very unusual improvisational technique. Previously we defined improvisation as a technique in which actors respond to each other during a performance in a manner which they believe appropriate to the characters they are portraying. In *My Hustler,* however, the actors say things that often have little relation to the roles they are acting or the "plot," but which are solely intended to "put on" the actor or actors they are playing against and to elicit certain responses from them—usually very humiliating or embarrassing. Thus, in *My Hustler* a "retired" male prostitute asks a young woman (who is obviously a virgin) whether or not she has ever had sexual relations with a man, simply for the sadistic pleasure he derives from watching her "squirm" out of giving a direct answer.*

---

* This "improvisational" technique can probably also be traced partly to Warhol's second period. For example, in *Screen Test Number Two* (1965), which is a put-on screen test for Mario Montez (in drag) conducted by Ronald Tavel, Mario is made to admit in the most humiliating way possible (for him) that he really is not a woman.

The films of Andy Warhol's fourth period were generally put together from separate half-hour takes* that featured different "superstars" from his growing repertory company, and which exploited in each case their exhibitionistic and pathetic attempts at self-degradation—each conglomerate of takes being projected simultaneously (by two different projectors) on a split screen. *Chelsea Girls* (1966), three-and-one-half hours long, and *Four Star* (1967), twenty-five hours long, comprise the major body of work for this period, with the former being by far the most successful (financially, at least) of the two. Somewhat like a Greenwich Village version of Dante's *Inferno*, *Chelsea Girls* is a stark semi-documentary in which male and female homosexuals, drug addicts and other related denizens of the New York sub-culture of which Andy Warhol is the chief chronicler all candidly bare their souls (and sometimes their bodies) before a cold, cynical camera that grinds on without mercy or pity. What distinguishes *Chelsea Girls* from other, more conventional documentaries on deviate life is Warhol's extraordinarily *blasé* attitude toward the sensational aspects of his subject-matter: Warhol keeps his camera constantly in motion with numerous pans and gratuitous zooms; and when the camera does finally come to a rest—usually for only an instant—it is, more often than not, on some extraneous, often unidentifiable, detail (is it a woman's thigh that we see, or just part of the kitchen sink?)—and all this while the sound track informs us of the numerous, bizarre and often violent activities that are purportedly taking place, but of which we rarely have even a glimpse. During his fourth period, it can be said that Andy Warhol has desensitized through his own apparent indifference what other documentary filmmakers would perhaps have singled out and emphasized for the shock value alone.

---

* A *take* is similar to what we previously termed a "sequence-shot"; it is a scene shot uninterruptedly, with the camera being turned off only at the end.

In *Four Star,* the second major work of this period and which chronologically follows *Chelsea Girls,* Warhol continues his exploration of the film medium: this time in a segment in which he experiments with the potentialities of color film stock (just as he did with black-and-white in *Empire*). Called "Sunset in California," this segment shows just what its title would indicate, a complete California sunset (lasting approximately forty-five minutes), which highlights the extraordinary color changes that it is possible to observe during one of nature's most beautiful events.

If it is possible to say that Andy Warhol's most recent films constitute a fifth period, it would be primarily because these films possess two very important characteristics that distinguish them from his earlier work: the employment of a very crude form of editing* (until recently Warhol's films were, for all practicable purposes, unedited) and the lack of his previous self-restraint in the handling of scenes of a frank, sexual nature, which has led to a few of his latest films bordering on pornography (e.g. *Blue Movie* [1969]—a film in which two garrulous people are graphically shown having sexual intercourse—has the dubious distinction of being one of the few films to be seized by the New York City police for being obscene and yet to have had that seizure upheld in the courts).

Most of these later Warhol films have been parodies of successful commercial *genres: Bike Boy* (1967) is a take-off on motorcycle films; *I, a Man* (1968) is a parody of the Danish sexploitation film *I, a Woman* (1966); and *Lonesome Cowboys* (1969) is a homosexual Western. All these films are made up of several loosely-related episodes which exten-

---

* This editing technique can be described as follows: if during the filming of a long take Warhol thinks that an improvisation is going badly, he turns off the camera until he feels that the performances of his non-actors has improved (in interest), which when projected on the screen looks like a jump cut (sometimes he may shut off the camera during a take simply to move it to a new position, which also presents the same effect when projected).

sively employ the put-on type of improvisation that we previously noted in some of his earlier works.

It is important to note that Andy Warhol has frequently collaborated with many different writers and directors—although the results of these collaborations are invariably billed as a "Warhol film," with frequently little or no credit going to his collaborators. One example is *Flesh* (1968), written and directed by Paul Morrissey, who is usually identified as Warhol's production manager and all-round "right-hand" man.* *Flesh* was made by Morrissey while Warhol was recovering from a gunshot wound inflicted by an irate actress (who had once appeared in one of his films). Starring Joe Dallesandro, it clearly takes its origin from Warhol's earlier *My Hustler,* since it too is about a male hustler who in this case is married to a woman who appears to be lesbian. In *Flesh*—which ran successfully in New York and, curiously, several large European cities—Morrissey deviated considerably from Warhol's usual formless structuring and made a rather crude attempt at plot development, story coherence and traditional editing; according to Parker Tyler,[17] this displeased Morrissey's then ailing mentor.

The surprising box-office success of *Flesh* must have indicated to Warhol and Morrissey the commercial potential of their previous subject matter; and their next film venture, *Trash* (1970)—which was an even bigger financial success than their former film—certainly bears this out. Also written and directed by Morrissey, *Trash* is a thorough commercialization of the Warhol *genre,* concerning the now very *clichéd* male hustler (again played by Joe Dallesandro) who, here impotent from the use of drugs, is a part-time burglar living in a filthy apartment on New York's Lower East Side with a female impersonator (played by Holly Woodlawn). In *Trash,* with its very contrived use of improvisation, the actors put on not only each other, as in earlier Warhol films, but the au-

---

* In this particular collaboration, Morrissey *did* receive full credit for his contributions.

dience as well. The result is that the film sometime resembles a raunchy replica of a late-night television talk show.

Women In Revolt (1972), the most recent Warhol production—again written and directed by Paul Morrissey—is a raunchy satire on Women's Liberation that features female impersonators Holly Woodlawn, Jackie Curtis and Candy Darling; it did not fare as well at the box-office as its two illustrious predecessors.

"Camp"

The films of Andy Warhol along with the Absurdist films of many other Underground filmmakers have sometimes been referred to—both in a derogative manner and in praise—as *camp*. *The American Heritage Dictionary of the English Language* (New York, American Heritage Publishing Co., 1969) defines "camp" as: (1) "An affectation or appreciation of manners and tastes commonly thought to be outlandish, vulgar, or banal"; and (2) "Banality or artificiality, when appreciated for its humor." Certainly many Underground films, including those of Andy Warhol, have been "outlandish, vulgar, or banal," while at the same time appreciated for their humor. However, if that were all there were to Underground films, I would not have called attention to them in this book. What the Underground has taught us, and specifically the early Warhol films, is to look at *comedy* in a new light.

The reader may have noted that I have hardly dealt with comedy at all in this book, and this is deliberate; in the recent post-war renaissance of the film, comedy has been sorely neglected. There have been a few notable exceptions like *8½* and Pietro Germi's brilliant satire *Divorce Italian Style* (*Divorzia all'italiana*, 1961) * but, by and large, film

---

* In the preface to his screenplay for *8½*, Fellini refers to his film as being a comedy, which it certainly is. In regard to *Divorce Italian Style*, I would have liked to have devoted a chapter to it; but because there is yet no published screenplay in English, I decided to abandon the idea, especially since that particular film's structure is so complex.

comedy has suffered of late, and for one ostensible reason—its lack of *humanity*. This deficiency, however, is not something new; it goes back to Aristotle's definition of comedy as the imitation of *inferior* persons—inferior, that is, to the audience. Considered in that light, how could comedy not suffer in the contemporary cinema? Especially when most serious films have been showing us how the most traditionally despicable characters—prostitutes, criminals, cowards, drug addicts, sex perverts—were also human beings. Thus, an above-ground Underground film, Robert Downey's *Putney Swope* (1969), in the worst tradition of college humor magazines, facilely shows how "inane" Madison Avenue and television commercials are, for the apparent purpose of making the filmmaker and the audience appear superior to the people who make and watch this so-called drivel (commercials). And in the later Paul Morrissey-Warhol films—e.g., *Flesh*, *Trash* and *Women in Revolt*—the drug addicts, homosexuals and transvestites that one tended to feel empathy with in their earlier films have become objects of ridicule.

However, not all Underground comedy has suffered from a superiority complex and/or was meant to hold up its subjects or actors to scorn. Certainly there have been, as we have already seen, many Underground films that were vicious parodies of Hollywood—the "parody," of course, being an important form of comedy—and certainly the makers of these films considered the Hollywood myth which they parodied something inferior and worthless—but only because they themselves had been gullible enough to have been taken in by the falsity of that myth. More often than not, laughter was obtained from the audience in Underground comedy not at the expense of the "actors" or subject matter, but at the expense of the filmmaker himself, who so candidly bared his tortured soul to us.

Parker Tyler notes[18] that within the Underground one can identify a particular variety of camp which is really a kind of satire that is funny "because it makes no effort to imitate anything well; rather it is a calculated semislander by a parodist with his own *sub rosa* personality to exploit." Tyler goes on to point out that in a *chic* parody—which is really the ultimate in the feeding of a superiority complex—it is necessary for there to be "a certain detachment from what is parodied; to exaggerate just enough to make the target amusingly ridiculous."

Yet Tyler finds that many Underground parodies cannot be considered *chic* because the parodists' imitations are usually the very opposite of detached—they are "*too* honest, *too* accurate." Thus, Tyler notes, although Mario Montez's impersonation of the late Maria Montez is "pretty bad" as far as female impersonations go, the real Undeground film buff would reply that "it is the beauty of the parody that the parodist is inept. Mario Montez does not impersonate Maria Montez; he 'is' (that is, wishes to *be*) Maria Montez." By those standards, it can easily be seen why the performances of female impersonators such as Holly Woodlawn and Candy Darling in Warhol's later films are so much inferior to the performances of Mario Montez in his earlier ones: their impersonations are too good, too polished—they are *tours de force* of mimicry; while that of Montez is a *tour de force* of being —being *human,* if indeed in a somewhat depraved way.

Perhaps Ronald Tavel had Mario Montez in mind when, in summing up the accomplishments of the New American Cinema, or Underground, he pointed to what he considered to be its badge: "its actors who stare into the camera suddenly as if about to wave to relatives, its blank overexposed footage, its purposeful amateurish put-together, its humanness."[19]

Summary, Some Recent Innovations and Conclusion

Our survey of the screenplay in the contemporary cinema and some of the more recent advances in film as an art was meant to show that cinema, and especially the screenplay from which it is usually derived, have equalled (if not in some cases surpassed) the subtleties and complexities that we usually associate with outstanding literature—all of which might very well support the thesis that cinema is, indeed, a recent *extension* of literature. We have seen how cinema (or film-making) is in fact one continuous creative process that can most logically be divided into three parts—writing, directing and editing—and which is more and more being performed (although not necessarily chronologically) by one person, popularly referred to as a "filmmaker." Our study also included an examination of the language of film—its syntax and structure—in which we saw how this language both resembles and differs from those of other related arts, noting especially how in the theatrical fiction film there is still a very heavy reliance on certain structures and conventions borrowed from literature and drama; and, relatedly, our examination pointed up certain important differences between cinema and literature, notably film's lack of a direct equivalent of the literary metaphor and its total visibility (i.e. unless the filmmaker in some way artistically intervenes, the camera will photograph *everything*). We also observed how the modern fiction film has evolved more from the tradition of the novel and its antecedents, going as far back as the epic poetry of Homer, than it has from the tradition of drama and the play (although film has borrowed heavily also from that form); as a corollary, we noted that many of the recent trends in film as regards subject matter, form and structure have come directly from literature: e.g. Realism, Naturalism, psychoanalysis, existentialism and the disjointed narrative. Having seen how cinema has borrowed heavily from literature, we then continued to see how it has equalled and surpassed it, especially in the representation and depiction of mental states and psychic activity: e.g. stream of consciousness, dreams, free association, non-verbal states of mind, etc. Most importantly, however, we observed how the majority of films and screenplays discussed in this book have deviated from long-accepted Aristotelian dramatic logic—that all plays must have a plot and that the essence of characterization is in the showing of a character making a moral choice (or choices); the films and screenplays studied here have, on the other hand, tended to be structured episodically, according to the everyday rhythm of life in some cases, and the characterizations in them have been effected primarily by having the characters make simple choices—e.g. the choice of a dress to wear or path to take for a walk—and not necessarily moral ones.

What is the nature of reality?

An important and recurring aesthetic question in this book has been "What is the nature of reality?" To some filmmakers, notably the neo-realists, "reality" is almost synonymous with "current events": one has only to "hunt it down in the streets," if even that much effort is necessary, "and turn the camera on it." However, for filmmakers such as Antonioni and Fellini, "reality" is something metaphysical, and thus more elusive—something that can only be seen indirectly or through the aid of special filters (the consciousness of the protagonists, the actions of the characters, or the incidents of the story) ; and if it is at all possible for reality to be seen directly by the filmmaker, he must first stylize and manipulate it before he can show it to his audience.

What makes a good screenplay?

We have studied many types of scripts in this book: scripts that have been very detailed and scripts that have been exceptionally sketchy and brief, serving merely as sheets of notes that the director will refer to when shooting his film—all of which points to the fact that the form and amount of detail to be found in a screenplay are usually dictated by the particular director and the working relationship between that director and the writer, if other than himself. However, despite their diversity, I do believe that the scripts studied in this book can provide us with some valid generalizations—especially the scripts of Michelangelo Antonioni and Federico Fellini—about the role of the scriptwriter (or the director when writing his own scripts) in contemporary films. First, the scriptwriter should realize that the screenplay represents only the initial stage in the making of a film; therefore, he should resist the temptation of taking over the director's functions, and, if he himself is the director, of jumping the gun so early in the game. Secondly, the writer should not intend that his script be complete in itself—as a full-blown work of art—otherwise, there would be little point in filming it. What the scriptwriter should be particularly concerned with at the writing stage is that his idea be fully thought out, that it can hold up on paper—for if it cannot, it will most assuredly fail to do so on film. Concomitantly, the action, structure and inner logic of the film should be completely understood and worked out by the writer at this time (of course, in films of a documentary nature it is not always possible or desirable to do so), along with the characters and dialogue—i.e. their purpose and meaning, respectively, but not necessarily their texture or exact details. Finally, the writer, in the final version of his script, should emphasize the depiction and description of the action—although not necessarily all or *any* of the individual shots, camera angles, etc.— for as Sergei Eisenstein remarked many years ago, a shooting script is "an instrument to transpose a fact, abstracted into a concept, back into a chain of concrete single actions . . ."[1] We must never forget that the filmmaker works with the concrete—those things that are capable of being registered on a film emulsion—not abstract ideas (although, as Eisenstein pointed out above, abstract ideas *can* be transposed by the filmmaker into concrete actions, objects, characters, etc.) .

New Innovations

There have been a few recent innovations in cinema (four to be exact) that I have not yet mentioned, primarily because either I did not think them important enough to merit the devotion of an entire chapter, or because there was no one representative film that I felt provided an example worthy of extensive analysis. The four innovations that I would now like to call attention to are as follows: the psychedelic film, the discursive film, the "cinema of ideas" and *cinéma-vérité*.

The psychedelic film, the discursive film and the "cinema of ideas"

We have seen how film has equalled and perhaps surpassed the novel as a medium for exploring or depicting mental states; one such state (or states) of mind that we have not previously mentioned is that which is induced by the taking of drugs. The depiction of drug-induced states of mind is really not so new to literature (e.g. William Burroughs's *The Naked Lunch,* an Arabian Nights sexual fantasy, was allegedly written while the author was under the influence of narcotics) or film (e.g. a little known example of the American *film noir, Murder My Sweet* [1944], has a sequence depicting the hallucinations of the protagonist, who has been given an unknown drug while unconscious; and there is the very famous *The Lost Weekend* [1945], which shows the hallucinations of the protagonist when under the influence of alcohol). However, a few recent films have concentrated on the depiction of hallucinations that are generated by the taking of various psychedelic drugs (e.g. LSD), such as *Chelsea Girls,* Roger Corman's *The Trip* (1967) and *Easy Rider* (1969). Films such as these have particularly tried to depict the bizarre mixtures of colors supposedly seen as hallucinations when under the influence of psychedelic drugs. Film has also recently demonstrated its possibilities in another manner once thought to be the exclusive domain of the novel—as a *discursive form.* The best example is perhaps Jean-Luc Godard's *Two or Three Things I Know About Her (Deux ou trois choses que je sais d'elle)* [1966], in which the director speaks very softly on the sound track (in a voice over) about his uncertainties in making this particular work.

This same film and his *La Chinoise* (1967) are examples of yet another trend of which Godard has been the foremost innovator: a *cinema of ideas,* in which ideas are not only presented but also explored. The idea for *Two or Three Things* came to Godard from a letter written to a Parisian newspaper concerning part-time prostitution by tenants living in new surburban high-rise apartment buildings; from this letter Godard fashioned his premise that to live in Paris today *(ca.* 1966), it is necessary to prostitute oneself in one way or another, and he explored this idea by means of his two protagonists: a couple living in one of these high-rise apartment buildings with the wife forced into part-time prostitution in order to make ends meet. In *La Chinoise,* Godard explores some of the ideas that are held by members of a Maoist-oriented student "cell" in Paris, from their sometimes unassailable logic to their utmost absurdity—e.g. suicide and murder. In contrast to these two very stimulating and thought-provoking works, Godard's latest work has primarily consisted of avowed Marxist "agi-prop" films (e.g. *See You at Mao* [1967] and *Pravda* [1970]), in which static and crude images are often accompanied by an off-screen commentator reading from Marx or some similarly-oriented author. When told by one interviewer that his latest films tended to be visually static and also rather didactic, Godard reportedly shrugged and replied that audiences have been given pretty images for too long: it was time that they were given words and ideas instead.

Cinéma-vérité

Cinéma-vérité ("cinema-truth") is a documentary approach to films most closely associated, in its beginnings, with French filmmakers Chris Marker and Jean Rouch;* it is a *genre* in which filmmakers—using new, lightweight portable equipment—unobtrusively (?) follow their subjects around recording uninterruptedly their actions. Two very important techniques are associated with this type of film: the use of non-actors and the direct interview. The first of these was also employed earlier, as we have already seen, by the neo-realist filmmakers in Italy; however, whereas they used non-

---

* Examples of some of these are: *Chronicle of a Summer* (*Chronique d'un été,* 1960–61) by Jean Rouch and Edgar Morin, a documentary about one summer in the lives of a disparate group of Parisians; *Le joli mai* (1962) by Chris Marker, another documentary about the lives led by Parisians, this time in the month of May; and *The Koumiko Mystery* (*Le Mystère Koumiko,* 1965), also by Chris Marker, a lyrical documentary about a lovely Japanese girl that the director met while filming the Olympic Games in Tokyo.

actors to portray similar people, the practitioners of *cinéma-verité* have used non-actors as *themselves* and not as actors. In the second technique—the direct interview—the filmmaker (off-screen in most cases) asks one or more of his subjects a series of questions, which sometimes can develop into a heated dialogue on trivial to important issues.

Cinéma-verité as a serious film style would probably have declined considerably in popularity, or at least reverted back to the conventional documentary from which it had evolved, had it chose, as neo-realism before it, to concentrate exclusively on the everyday lives of everyday people, because, as the practitioners of this new type of cinema soon found out, everyday people when portraying themselves are just as dull, just as self-conscious and inhibited, and make just as bad actors as when they are called upon to portray persons other than themselves. However, as the filmmakers of this school— and particularly those in America*—turned their attention more and more to less ordinary and, in some cases, bizarre and sensational subjects—e.g. politicians, showmen, pompous entertainers, homosexuals, drug addicts and mental patients —they began to discover, as did their audiences, that contrary to what had been the experience of Italian neo-realism and the early *cinéma-verité* films, there were a considerable number of people (non-actors) who, when put before a movie camera, not only acted *naturally*, but in many instances cavorted or brazenly bared their souls as if either the camera were not there, or, conversely, expressly for its benefit like exhibitionists (we have previously mentioned a few examples of this type of non-actor in our discussion of the semi-documentaries of Andy Warhol).

Surprisingly enough, *cinéma-verité* has had an inordinate

---

* We have already mentioned some of these filmmakers—e.g. Ricky Leacock, Morris Engel and Don Pennebaker—in regard to the so-called New York school (see Chapter Twelve); however, their approach to *cinéma-verité* tended to be less lyrical and stylized than their European counterparts, while at the same time eschewing any kind of narration whatsoever.

amount of influence on narrative filmmaking. The reason for this is probably related to a desire of fiction filmmakers to endow their films with a greater degree of reality, which is closely related to the recent world-wide revolt against the traditional methods of movie making that we have already mentioned. This influence has demonstrated itself in many ways: for instance, there have been fiction films that have tried to emulate the most common *cinéma-vérité* form and structure—following the film's subject around with a camera wherever that subject goes and for a specified period of time. Agnès Varda's *Cleo from 5 to 7* (*Cléo de 5 à 7*, 1962) is such an example, supposedly two hours filmed from the life of the heroine (Cleo) at the end of which time she is to learn from her doctor whether or not she has cancer. This film, which in actuality is only about an hour-and-a-half long, contains many incidents that are typical of *cinéma-vérité* films: e.g. a journey in a taxi-cab, a ride on a bus, shopping for a new hat and a walk through a park. There are also films in which professional actors go out of their way to pretend that they are not actually delivering lines—e.g. overlapping dialogue, stammering and, in some cases, even mumbling—and, as a corollary, there are films in which the director will deliberately use very crude methods to film a pre-written and pre-rehearsed scene, e.g. a hand-held camera and a poorly-placed (for a sound pickup) microphone—ostensibly to make the scene appear more spontaneous than it in fact is. Other examples of *cinéma-vérité* in fiction films are scenes in which the main characters are photographed in real crowds, parades and even riots. There have also been films in which the actors or filmmaker conducts interviews with real people, or the actors themselves are interviewed by the filmmaker—sometimes discussing their roles with him.

The reader may have been given the impression that I am not very impressed with the use of *cinéma-vérité* techniques in fiction films. Truthfully, I have only seen one such film in which I believe that these techniques were at all well integrated: Jean-Luc Godard's *Masculine-Feminine* (*Masculin-Féminin*, 1965) —and perhaps in a few parts, Haskell Wexler's *Medium Cool* (1969), which is centered around the infamous 1968 Democratic National Convention. It appears that in most such films the fictional techniques—e.g. plot, characters and dialogue—do not mix well with the *cinéma-vérité* techniques employed, and often it is hard to tell in these instances which of the two techniques (fictional or *cinéma vérité*) is at fault. I would venture to guess that in many of these films the filmmakers themselves were basically uncertain as to whether or not a plot is a falsification of life—as was proposed several years ago by Cesare Zavattini—or a sometimes useful tool for capturing reality.

Salesman (*1967*)

Before we conclude this brief discussion of *cinéma-vérité*, I would like to examine one such film of this *genre*, from its conception to its completion, in order that we may at least get a minimal exposure to how this type of film differs from the other kinds studied in this book—in fact, the difference is not that great, for the *cinéma-vérité* film, just like the others, is also the result of a creative process that involves writing (or thinking), filming and editing, only here there is a much greater emphasis on the latter two stages. The film that I have selected for this purpose is *Salesman*, conceived and directed by Albert and David Maysles, who were assisted in the editing by Charlotte Zwerin; it is primarily the story of four door-to-door Bible salesmen struggling to make a living, and is not without its share of poignancy, pathos and humor. The filmmakers had previously been associated with the *cinéma-vérité* movement in the United States that grew out of the New York school in the early Sixties; however, according to Howard Junker in the "Production Notes" for the published text of *Salesman*,[2] the two brothers had become rather disillusioned with the sensational, bigger-than-life dramas that were increasingly becoming the mainstay of this type of documentary film production: they believed, instead, that a documentary film—even one that was feature-length—could be successfully made about everyday people doing only everyday things (not too different from Cesare Zavattini's goal).* After having conducted a long and extensive search for such a subject, the two brothers finally settled on the idea of making a film about salesmen—partially influenced in their selection by the sympathetic treatment of this subject in Eugene O'Neill's play *The Iceman Cometh*—and choosing for this purpose four Bible salesmen who were working out of Boston at the time. The Maysles then followed their four subjects to their new sales territory in Florida, and into the homes of their prospective customers. Surprisingly, of all the households approached by the four salesmen—who were accompanied at all times by both a cameraman and soundman (the two brothers themselves) and their portable equipment—less than ten per cent refused to allow any filming to take place at all, according to Howard Junker; and after filming, only one person refused to grant the filmmakers permission to use the segments in which they had just appeared. The filming took the Maysles brothers approximately six weeks to complete and comprised, originally, some thirty hours of footage, which, after fifteen months of editing, was boiled down to a rough assembly one-and-a-half hours long. During further refining, the film's "plot" slowly began to develop: instead of having the film focus on the four salesmen equally, one of the salesmen, Paul, began to emerge as the dominant character—a salesman who, according to David Maysles, can't make it in his profession because he has more soul than his more successful colleagues.[3]

Cinéma-vérité has, at the very least, provided us with some very exciting footage; however, whether or not it can really be considered as an *artistic* approach to film, some doubts

---

* The Maysles brothers prefer to call their particular approach to filmmaking "direct cinema," instead of *cinéma-vérité*.

may still linger. For example, it is not always clear in many examples of this *genre* where the dividing line between journalism and art is, if indeed there is any at all. Also, it appears that all too frequently the *cinéma-vérité* filmmaker is almost totally dependent on external events or conditions for the structure of the film itself—with direction in many such instances being nothing more than a matter of logistics: being at the right place at the right time. I, for one, believe that *cinéma-vérité* will continue to play an important role in the development of film as an art; but, on the other hand, the most eloquent statement of this *genre* has yet to be made.

Conclusion

And so this study of the modern screenplay and its relation to the creative process of filmmaking and film as art comes to a close. What the future may hold for the medium—and for screenwriting in particular—no one can really say; hopefully it will continue to flourish. Certainly the way to further achievements has been brilliantly illuminated by the personal contributions of such noteworthy writers and writer-directors as Bergman, Zavattini, Godard, Fellini and Antonioni; it only remains for us to follow in their paths.

Appendix A
Text References

Introduction

1. *Twenty Best Film Plays,* John Gassner and Dudley Nichols, eds. (New York, Crown Publishers, 1943).
2. Alexandre Astruc, "La Camera-Stylo," reprinted and translated in *"The New Wave,"* Peter Graham, ed. (Garden City, N.Y., Doubleday & Company, 1968), pp. 17–18.
3. *Ibid.,* p. 19.
4. *Ibid.,* p. 20.
5. *Ibid.,* p. 22.
6. Quoted in "Interview with François Truffaut," *Cahiers du Cinéma,* Paris, No. 138 (1962), reprinted and translated in *The New Wave,* p. 92.
7. Quoted in "An Interview with Jean-Luc Godard," *Cahiers du Cinéma,* Paris (Dec., 1962), reprinted in *Jean-Luc Godard,* Toby Mussman, ed., trans. by Rose Kaplin (New York, E. P. Dutton & Co., 1968), p. 110.
8. Statement attributed to Jacques Rivette concerning his film *Paris nous appartient* (1960). Quoted in Gérard Gozlan, "In Praise of André Bazin," *Positif,* Paris, No. 47 (1962), reprinted and translated in *The New Wave,* pp. 118–19.
9. André Bazin, *What Is Cinema?,* ed. and trans. by Hugh Gray (Berkeley and Los Angeles, University of California Press, 1967), p. 56.

Chapter 1: The Language of Film

1. Rouben Mamoulian, "Colour and Light in Films," *Film Culture*, New York, No. 21 (Summer 1960), pp. 74–75.
2. Michelangelo Antonioni, *Screenplays of Michelangelo Antonioni*, trans. by Louis Brigante and Roger J. Moore (New York, The Orion Press, 1963), pp. XVII–XVIII.
3. Andrew Sarris, "Notes on the Auteur Theory in 1962," *Film Culture*, New York, No. 27 (Winter 1962–63), pp. 1–8.
4. *Ibid.*, p. 7.
5. *Ibid.*
6. Alexandre Astruc, "What Is Mise-en-Scène?" *Film Culture*, New York, No. 22–23 (Summer 1961), p. 65.

Chapter 2: Dramaturgy

1. John Howard Lawson, *Film: The Creative Process*, 2nd ed. (New York, Hill and Wang, 1964), p. 340.

Chapter 3: The Narrative in Cinema: Film's Debt to the Novel

1. Ben Hecht, *A Child of the Century* (New York, Simon and Schuster, 1954), pp. 488–89.
2. John Gassner, "Reprise for the Film Plays," *Great Film Plays*, John Gassner and Dudley Nichols, eds. (New York, Crown Publishers, 1959), p. VIII.
3. George Bluestone, *Novels into Film* (Berkeley and Los Angeles, University of California Press, 1957), pp. 47–48.
4. Pier Paolo Pasolini, "Cinematic and Literary Stylistic Figures," *Film Culture*, New York, No. 24 (Spring 1962), p. 42.
5. *Ibid.*
6. Ingmar Bergman, *Four Screenplays of Ingmar Bergman*, trans. by Lars Malmström and David Kushner (New York, Simon and Schuster, 1960), p. XVII. Italics my own.
7. Pasolini, *op. cit.*, p. 42.
8. *Ibid.*
9. André Bazin, *What Is Cinema?*, ed. and trans. by Hugh Gray (Berkeley and Los Angeles, University of California Press, 1967), p. 68.

Chapter 4: The Classic American Screenplay

1. Robert Gessner, *The Moving Image* (New York, E. P. Dutton & Co., 1968), pp. 55–59.
2. *Ibid.*, pp. 85–93.
3. *Ibid.*, p. 88.
4. *Ibid.*, p. 48.
5. Robert Warshow, "The Westerner," *The Immediate Experience* (Garden City, N.Y., Doubleday & Co., 1968), p. 139.

6. *Ibid.*, p. 142.
7. *Ibid.*, p. 143.
8. *Ibid.*, p. 153.
9. Included in André Bazin, *What Is Cinema?*, ed. and trans. by Hugh Gray (Berkeley and Los Angeles, University of California Press, 1967).
10. *Ibid.*, p. 36.

Chapter 5: Neo-Realism and the Nature of Reality
1. Eric Rhode, "Why Neo-Realism Failed," *Sight and Sound*, London, Vol. 30, No. 1 (Winter 1960–61), p. 27.
2. Penelope Houston, *The Contemporary Cinema* (Baltimore, Penguin Books, 1963), p. 19.
3. *Ibid.*, p. 20.
4. Quoted in the program notes (unsigned) for "An Evening with Cesare Zavattini," The Museum of Modern Art, New York, N.Y. (May 13, 1969).
5. Quoted in Rhode, *op. cit.*, p. 28.
6. John Howard Lawson, *Film: The Creative Process*, 2nd ed. (New York, Hill and Wang, 1964), p. 340.
7. *Ibid.*, p. 150.
8. Houston, *op. cit.*, p. 26.
9. "An Evening with Cesare Zavattini."
10. Cesare Zavattini, "Some Ideas on the Cinema," trans. by Pier Luigi Lanza, *Sight and Sound*, London, Vol. 23, No. 2 (October–December, 1953), p. 67.
11. *Ibid.*, pp. 65–66.
12. *Ibid.*, p. 66.
13. *Ibid.*
14. *Ibid.*, p. 64.

Chapter 6: Diary of a Country Priest: Robert Bresson and the Literary Adaptation
1. André Bazin, *What Is Cinema?*, ed. and trans. by Hugh Gray (Berkeley and Los Angeles, University of California Press, 1967), pp. 56–57.
2. Margaret Kennedy, *The Mechanized Muse* (London, George Allen & Unwin, 1942), p. 29.
3. Bazin, *op. cit.*, p. 128.
4. *Ibid.*
5. Georges Bernanos, *The Diary of a Country Priest*, trans. by Pamela Morris (New York, The Macmillan Co., 1937), p. 203.
6. Ernest Lindgren, *The Art of the Film*, revised ed. (New York, The Macmillan Co., 1963), pp. 109–110.
7. John Russell Taylor, *Cinema Eye, Cinema Ear* (New York, Hill and Wang, 1964), p. 125.

8. *Ibid.*, p. 126.
9. *Ibid.*, p. 127.
10. *Ibid.*, p. 128.
11. *Ibid.*
12. Bazin, *op. cit.*, p. 134.
13. *Ibid.*, pp. 134–35.
14. *Ibid.*, p. 140.
15. *Ibid.*
16. *Ibid.*, p. 142.

Chapter 7: Wild Strawberries: A Dream Play

1. Ingmar Bergman, *Four Screenplays of Ingmar Bergman*, trans. by Lars Malmström and David Kushner (New York, Simon and Schuster, 1960), p. XVII.
2. Jörn Donner, *The Personal Vision of Ingmar Bergman*, trans. by Holger Lurdbergh (Bloomington, Indiana University Press, 1964), pp. 153–54. This observation was originally made in Frederic Durand, "Ingmar Bergman et la littérature suédoise," *Cinéma 60*, No. 47 (June, 1960).
3. Peter Cowie, *Three Monographs: Antonioni, Bergman, Resnais* (London, Tantivy Press/New York, A. S. Barnes & Co., 1963).
4. *Ibid.*, p. 64.
5. Donner, *op. cit.*, p. 157.
6. *Ibid.*, p. 165.
7. Birgitta Steene, *Ingmar Bergman* (New York, Twayne Publishers, Inc., 1968), p. 71.
8. Bergman, *op. cit.*, p. 233.
9. Cowie, *op. cit.*, p. 96.
10. Bergman, *op. cit.*, p. 238.
11. Eugene Archer, "*Wild Strawberries*," *Film Quarterly*, Berkeley, Vol. XII (Fall 1959), p. 44.
12. Steene, *op. cit.*, p. 72.
13. Donner, *op. cit.*, p. 159.
14. Bergman, *op. cit.*, p. 169.
15. *Ibid.*, p. 228.
16. *Ibid.*, p. 227.
17. *Ibid.*
18. *Ibid.*, p. 212.
19. *Ibid.*, p. 223.
20. August Strindberg, *Six Plays of Strindberg*, trans. by Elizabeth Sprigge (Garden City, N.Y., Doubleday & Co., 1955), p. 193. The importance of Strindberg's *A Dream Play* to an understanding of *Wild Strawberries* is also noted by Birgitta Steene and Jörn Donner in the works cited above.
21. Bergman, *op. cit.*, p. 232.

22. Sigmund Freud, *An Outline of Psycho-analysis,* trans. by James Strachey (New York, W. W. Norton & Co., 1949) , p. 61.

23. Bergman, *op. cit.,* p. 182.

24. Archer, *op. cit.,* p. 44.

25. Bergman, *op. cit.,* p. 213.

26. *Ibid.,* p. 217.

27. Stanley Kauffmann, *A World on Film* (New York, Harper & Row, Publishers, 1966) , p. 271.

28. Bergman, *op. cit.*

29. *Ibid.,* p. XV.

30. *Ibid.,* p. XVI.

31. *Ibid.*

32. *Ibid.,* p. XVII.

33. *Ibid.*

Chapter 8: Stream of Consciousness in the Novel and Film

1. William James, *Principles of Psychology* (New York, Henry Holt and Co., 1890) , p. 239.

2. *Ibid.*

3. Sigmund Freud, *The Interpretation of Dreams,* ed. and trans. by James Strachey, Standard ed. (New York, Basic Books, 1953) , p. 102.

4. *Ibid.*

5. James Joyce, *Ulysses* (New York, Vintage Books, 1934) , p. 738.

6. Quoted in Robert Humphrey, *Stream of Consciousness in the Modern Novel* (Berkeley and Los Angeles, University of California Press, 1954) , p. 31.

7. *Ibid.,* p. 34.

8. Sergei Eisenstein, *Film Form,* trans. by Jay Leyda (Cleveland and New York, The World Publishing Co. [Meridian], 1957) , p. 246.

9. *Ibid.,* p. 245.

10. *Ibid.,* p. 252.

11. *Ibid.,* p. 242.

12. *Ibid.*

13. *Ibid.,* p. 106.

14. *Ibid.,* p. 130.

15. *Ibid.,* p. 144.

16. *Ibid.,* pp. 144–45.

17. *Ibid.,* p. 145.

18. *Ibid.,* p. 103.

19. *Ibid.,* p. 103–104.

20. *Ibid.,* p. 103.

21. *Ibid.*

22. *Ibid.,* p. 105.

Chapter 9: Existentialism and the Anti-Hero in Cinema
1. Raymond Borde and Etienne Chaumeton, *Un Panorama du film noir américain* (Paris, Les Editions de Minuit, 1955), pp. 4–5.
2. Quoted in "An Interview with Jean-Luc Godard," *Cahiers du Cinéma*, Paris (Dec., 1962), reprinted in *Jean-Luc Godard*, Toby Mussman, ed., trans. by Rose Kaplin (New York, E. P. Dutton & Co., 1968), p. 105.
3. Jean-Luc Godard, *Le Petit Soldat*, trans. by Nicholas Garnham (London, Lorrimer Publishing, 1967), p. 22.
4. *Ibid.*, p. 69.
5. *Ibid.*, p. 48.
6. *Ibid.*, p. 79.
7. *Ibid.*, p. 20.
8. Quoted in Jean Collet, *Jean-Luc Godard*, trans. by Ciba Vaughan (New York, Crown Publishers, 1970), p. 92.
9. "An Interview with Jean-Luc Godard," p. 108.

Chapter 10: Federico Fellini and the Psychoanalytic Technique in Film
1. Federico Fellini, Tullio Pinelli, Ennio Flaiano, and Brunello Rondi, *Juliet of the Spirits*, Tullio Kezich, ed., trans. by Howard Greenfield (New York, Ballantine Books, 1966), p. 24.
2. *Ibid.*, p. 30.
3. *Ibid.*, pp. 26–27.
4. *Ibid.*, p. 49.
5. *Ibid.*, p. 21.
6. *Ibid.*, p. 40.
7. *Ibid.*
8. *Ibid.*, p. 42.
9. Quoted in Jill Neville and Angelo Quattrocchi, "Fellini's *Satyricon;* A Pagan *Dolce Vita:* 'Faces Are My Words,'" *The Village Voice*, New York (January 22, 1970), p. 57.
10. Fellini, *op. cit.*, p. 40.
11. *Ibid.*
12. *Ibid.*, p. 39.
13. *Ibid.*, pp. 40–41.
14. *Ibid.*, p. 39.
15. *Ibid.*, p. 47.
16. Robert Gessner, *The Moving Image* (New York, E. P. Dutton & Co., 1968), p. 259.
17. Fellini, *op. cit.*, p. 23.
18. *Ibid.*, p. 57.
19. *Ibid.*, p. 62.
20. *Ibid.*, p. 54.
21. *Ibid.*, p. 46.

22. *Ibid.*, p. 194.
23. *Ibid.*, p. 45.
24. *Ibid.*, pp. 300–301.
25. *Ibid.*, p. 250.
26. *Ibid.*, p. 313.
27. *Ibid.*, p. 315.
28. *Ibid.*, p. 317.
29. *Ibid.*, p. 318.
30. *Ibid.*, p. 174.
31. *Ibid.*, p. 35.
32. *Ibid.*
33. Gessner, *op. cit.*, p. 400.

Chapter 11: Antonioni and the Plotless Screenplay

1. Michelangelo Antonioni, "A Talk with Michelangelo Antonioni on His Work," *Film Culture*, New York, No. 24 (Spring 1962), p. 46.
2. Michelangelo Antonioni, "Making a Film is My Way of Life," *Film Culture*, New York, No. 24 (Spring 1962), p. 44.
3. Quoted in Pierre Leprohon, *Michelangelo Antonioni*, trans. by Scott Sullivan (New York, Simon and Schuster, 1963), p. 25.
4. *Ibid.*, pp. 26–27.
5. "A Talk with Michelangelo Antonioni on His Work," p. 48.
6. Antonioni, "Making a Film is My Way of Life," p. 45.
7. Quoted in Leprohon, *op. cit.*, p. 96.
8. "A Talk with Michelangelo Antonioni on His Work," p. 47.
9. Quoted in Leprohon, *op. cit.*, p. 62.
10. *Ibid.*
11. *Ibid.*, p. 65.
12. *Ibid.*, p. 77.
13. "A Talk with Michelangelo Antonioni on His Work," p. 61.
14. Michelangelo Antonioni, *Screenplays of Michelangelo Antonioni*, trans. by Louis Brigante and Roger J. Moore (New York, The Orion Press, 1963), p. 262.
15. Quoted in Leprohon, *op. cit.*, p. 30.
16. Antonioni, *Screenplays*, p. 273.
17. "A Talk with Michelangelo Antonioni on His Work," p. 53.
18. Antonioni, *Screenplays*, pp. 219–20.
19. *Ibid.*, pp. 223–27.
20. Quoted in Leprohon, *op. cit.*, p. 162.
21. "A Talk with Michelangelo Antonioni on His Work," p. 47.
22. Antonioni, *Screenplays*, p. 225.
23. Quoted in Leprohon, *op. cit.*, p. 95.

24. Michelangelo Antonioni and Monca Vitti, *"Eclipse," Theatre Arts,* New York (July, 1962) , p. 7.
25. *Ibid.*
26. Stanley Kauffman, *A World on Film* (New York, Harper & Row, Publishers, 1966) , p. 310.
27. Antonioni, *Screenplays,* p. 352.
28. "A Talk with Michelangelo Antonioni on His Work," p. 54.
29. Quoted in Robert Gessner, *The Moving Image* (New York, E. P. Dutton & Co., 1968) , p. 398. Italics my own.
30. *Ibid.,* p. 397.
31. *Ibid.,* p. 399.
32. Antonioni, *Screenplays,* p. IX.
33. *Ibid.,* p. X.
34. *Ibid.,* pp. XIV–XV.
35. *Ibid.,* p. XVIII.
36. "A Talk with Michelangelo Antonioni on His Work," p. 48.
37. *Ibid.*

Chapter 12: The Underground Cinema

1. Quoted in "An Interview with Jean-Luc Godard," *Cahiers du Cinéma,* Paris (Dec., 1962) , reprinted in *Jean-Luc Godard,* Toby Mussman, ed., trans. by Rose Kaplin (New York, E. P. Dutton & Co., 1968) , p. 119.
2. "The First Statement of the New American Cinema Group," *Film Culture,* New York, Nos. 22–23 (Summer 1961) , pp. 131–133.
3. Jonas Mekas, "Notes on the New American Cinema," *Film Culture,* New York, No. 24 (Spring 1962) , p. 13.
4. Quoted in *Film-Makers' Co-operative Catalogue No. 3,* reprinted in *Film Culture,* New York, No. 37 (Summer 1965) , p. 52.
5. *Film Culture,* New York, No. 29 (Summer 1963) , p. 1.
6. Ronald Tavel, "The Banana Diary," *Film Culture,* New York, No. 40 (Spring 1966) , pp. 49–50.
7. *Ibid.,* p. 44.
8. *Ibid.,* p. 50.
9. Quoted in Sheldon Renan, "Interview with the Kuchar Brothers," *Film Culture,* New York, No. 45 (Summer 1967) , p. 49.
10. Sheldon Renan, *An Introduction to the American Underground Film* (New York, E. P. Dutton & Co., 1967) , p. 191.
11. Gerard Malanga, "Let's Be Serious: A Portrait of Baby Jane Holzer," *Film Culture,* New York, No. 45 (Summer 1967) , p. 36.
12. David Ehrenstein, "An Interview with Andy Warhol," *Film Culture,* New York, No. 40 (Spring 1966) , p. 41.
13. "An Interview with Jean-Luc Godard," p. 104.

14. Gregory Battcock, "Notes on Empire: A Film by Andy Warhol," *Film Culture*, New York, No. 40 (Spring 1966), p. 40.
15. *Ibid.*, p. 39.
16. *Film Culture*, New York, No. 33 (Summer 1964), p. 1.
17. Parker Tyler, *Underground Film: A Critical History* (New York, Grove Press, Inc., 1969), p. 22.
18. *Ibid.*, pp. 46–47.
19. Tavel, *op. cit.*, p. 44.

Summary, Some Recent Innovations, and Conclusion

1. Sergei Eisenstein, *Film Form* (Cleveland and New York, The World Publishing Company [Meridian], 1957), p. 138.
2. The Maysles Brothers, *Salesman* (New York, The New American Library [Signet], 1969), pp. 106–107.
3. *Ibid.*, p. 120.

Appendix B
Selected Bibliography

Books:

There have been a number of fine works on film that were of assistance to me in the preparation of this book, and reference has been made to many of them in Appendix A; however, the reader may find the following four books of particular interest, since they all, to some degree, approach film as a narrative art— the primary emphasis of this book.

Bazin, André, *What Is Cinema?*, Vol. I, ed. and trans. by Hugh Gray. Berkeley and Los Angeles, University of California Press, 1967.

Eisenstein, Sergei, *Film Form* and *Film Sense,* trans. by Jay Leyda. Cleveland and New York, The World Publishing Company (Meridian), 1957.

Gessner, Robert, *The Moving Image.* New York, E. P. Dutton & Co., 1968.

Lawson, John Howard, *Film: The Creative Process,* 2nd ed. New York, Hill and Wang, 1964.

Screenplays:

The following is a fairly complete list of screenplays published in English which, I believe, may be of interest to the readers of this book. Although some of the screenplays listed below are out of print, they may be available at public, university and museum libraries, and bookstores specializing in out-of-print books.* To ascertain whether a particular screenplay is in print, the reader should consult *Books in Print* (published by R. R. Bowker Co., 1180 Avenue of the Americas, New York, N.Y. 10036), and for a more thorough listing of screenplays published in paperback editions (which most are), he should consult *Paperbound Books in Print* (also from the same publisher).

The list has been divided into three categories: American, British, and foreign. These categories refer primarily to the language or country of origin of the films made from the listed screenplays and do not necessarily indicate the nationality of the screenwriter or director, with the last category designating primarily those films made in non-English speaking countries—even though, in some instances, made in English. (I realize, however, that the reader may find my classification of certain films rather arbitrary, especially in instances of international co-productions.)

American

Agee, James, *Agee on Film* (*Vol. II*) : *Five Film Plays by James Agee.* New York, Grosset & Dunlop Publishers, 1969. Includes the following screenplays: *Noa Noa, The African Queen, The Night of the Hunter, The Bride Comes to Yellow Sky,* and *The Blue Hotel.*

Anderson, Maxwell, and Solt, Andrew, *Joan of Arc.* New York, Sloane Publishers, 1948.

Anderson, Robert, *I Never Sang for My Father,* New York, The New American Library (Signet), 1970.

Beckett, Samuel, *Film.* New York, Grove Press, 1969.

Capote, Truman, and Perry, Eleanor, *Trilogy: An Experiment in Multimedia.* New York, The Macmillan Company, 1969. Contains the following short stories by Truman Capote, plus the screenplays adapted from them: *Miriam, Among the Paths to Eden,* and *A Christmas Memory.*

---

* For an extensive listing of bookstores—throughout the world—specializing in out-of-print film books consult the annual *International Film Guide,* Peter Cowie, ed. (London, Tantivy Press/New York, A. S. Barnes & Co.) .

Carson, L. M. Kit, *David Holzman's Diary*. New York, Farrar, Straus and Giroux, 1970.

Cassavetes, John, *Faces*. New York, The New American Library (Signet), 1970.
Includes both the original screenplay and a transcription of the final film.

Chayefsky, Paddy, *The Bachelor Party*. New York, The New American Library (Signet), 1955.

————, *The Goddess*. New York, Simon and Schuster, 1958.

Downey, Robert, *Chafed Elbows*. New York, Lancer Books, 1967.

Eastman, Charles, *All American Boy*. New York, Farrar, Straus and Giroux (Noonday), 1971.

————, *Little Fauss and Big Halsy*. New York, Farrar, Straus and Giroux (Noonday), 1970.

Fast, Howard Melvin, *The Hill*. Garden City, N.Y., Doubleday & Co., Inc., 1964.

Fonda, Peter; Hopper, Dennis; and Southern, Terry; *Easy Rider*. New York, The New American Library (Signet), 1969.

Foote, Horton, *To Kill a Mockingbird*. New York, Harcourt, Brace & World, Inc., 1962.

Ford, John, *Stagecoach*. New York, Simon and Schuster, 1971.

Fowler, Gene, and Meredyth, Bess, *The Mighty Barnum*. New York, Covici-Friede, 1934.

Garret, George P.; Gelfan, Jane; and Hardison, O. B., Jr., eds., *Film Scripts* Vol. I. New York, Appleton-Century-Crofts, 1971. *Henry V, The Big Sleep,* and *A Streetcar Named Desire*.

————, *Film Scripts* Vol. II. New York, Appleton-Century-Crofts, 1971. *High Noon, Twelve Angry Men,* and *The Defiant Ones*.

Gassner, John, and Nichols, Dudley, eds., *Best Film Plays of 1943–1944*. New York, Crown Publishers, Inc., 1945.
Includes the following screenplays: *Wilson, The Purple Heart, The Miracle of Morgan's Creek, Going My Way, Watch on the Rhine, Dragon Seed, The More the Merrier, Hail the Conquering Hero, The Ox-Bow Incident,* and *Casablanca*.

————, *Best Film Plays of 1945*. New York, Crown Publishers, 1946.
Includes the following screenplays: *The Machine from the God, The Lost Weekend, Spellbound, Double Indemnity,*

A Tree Grows in Brooklyn, None but the Lonely Heart, The Southerner, The Story of G. I. Joe, Thirty Seconds Over Tokyo, Over Twenty-One, and *A Medal for Benny.*

————, *Great Film Plays.* New York, Crown Publishers, 1943.
Includes the following screenplays: *It Happened One Night, Rebecca, The Life of Emile Zola, The Good Earth, All That Money Can Buy,* and *Stagecoach.*

————, *Twenty Best Film Plays.* New York, Crown Publishers, Inc., 1943.
Includes all of the screenplays listed above for *Great Film Plays,* plus the following: *The Women, My Man Godfrey, Here Comes Mr. Jordan, Wuthering Heights, The Grapes of Wrath, How Green Was My Valley, Make Way for Tomorrow, Little Caesar, Fury, Mr. Smith Goes to Washington, Juarez, Mrs. Miniver, This Land Is Mine, Yellow Jack,* and *The Fight for Life.*

Ginsberg, Milton Moses, *Coming Apart.* New York, Lancer Books, 1969.

Goldman, William, *Butch Cassidy and the Sundance Kid.* New York, Bantam Books, 1969.

Hellman, Lillian, *The North Star.* New York, The Viking Press, 1943.

Hellman, Sam, and Long, Hal, *Stanley and Livingstone.* Beverly Hills, Calif., 20th Century-Fox Film Corp., 1937.

Herndon, Venable, and Penn, Arthur, *Alice's Restaurant.* Garden City, N.Y., Doubleday & Co., 1970.

Hutchins, Robert M., *Zuckerkandl.* New York, Grove Press, 1968.

Jennings, Talbot, *Romeo and Juliet.* New York, Random House, 1936.

Kubrick, Stanley, *Clockwork Orange.* New York, Ballantine Books, Inc., 1972.
This is the transcription of the final film, which was based on the novel of the same name by Anthony Burgess.

Lewis, Sinclair, and Schary, Dore, *Storm in the West.* New York, Stein and Day, 1963.

Mankiewicz, Joseph I., *All about Eve.* New York, Random House, 1951.

Maysles Brothers (David and Albert), and Zwerin, Charlotte, *Salesman.* New York, The New American Library (Signet), 1969.

This is a transcription of the final film.

Miller, Arthur, *The Misfits.* New York, The Viking Press, 1961.

Nichols, Dudley, *The Informer.* Included in Theatre Arts, New York, Vol. XXXV, No. 8 (August, 1951).

Pennebaker, D. A., *Don't Look Back.* New York, Ballantine Books, Inc., 1968.
This is a transcription of the final film.

Perry, Eleanor, *The Swimmer.* New York, Stein and Day, 1967.

Schulberg, Budd, *Across the Everglades.* New York, Random House, 1958.

———, *A Face in the Crowd.* New York, Random House, Inc., 1967.

Steinbeck, John, *The Forgotten Village.* New York, The Viking Press, Inc., 1941.

Tavel, Ronald, and Warhol, Andy, *Harlot.* Included in *Film Culture,* New York, No. 40 (Spring 1966).
This is a transcription of the soundtrack of the final film.

Thompson, Robert E., *They Shoot Horses, Don't They?* Included in the reissue of Horace McCoy's novel of the same title. New York, Avon Publishers, 1969.

von Stroheim, Erich, *Greed.* New York, Simon and Schuster, 1971.

Warhol, Andy, *Blue Movie.* New York, Grove Press, 1970.
This is a transcription of the final film.

Welles, Orson and Mankiewicz, Herman, *Citizen Kane.* Complete shooting script included in *The Citizen Kane Book* by Pauline Kael. Boston, Little, Brown & Co., 1971.

Wexler, Norman, *Joe.* New York, Avon Books, 1970.

Wilder, Billy, and Diamond, I. A. L., *Two Screenplays: The Apartment* and *The Fortune Cookie.* New York, Praeger Publishers, 1971.

Williams, Tennessee, *Baby Doll.* New York, New Directions Publishing Corporation, 1956.

Wilson, Michael, *Salt of the Earth.* Included in the book with the same title by Biberman, Herbert. Boston, Beacon Press, 1965.

British
Anderson, Lindsay, and Sherwin, David, *If . . .* New York, Simon and Schuster, 1969.

The screenplay was actually written by John Howlett and David Sherwin; Lindsay Anderson was the director.

Biró, Lajos, and Wimperis, Arthur, *The Private Life of Henry VIII*. London, Methuen & Co., 1934.

Bolt, Robert, *Doctor Zhivago*. New York, Random House, 1965.

Brogger, Frederick, and Pulman, Jack, *David Copperfield*. Included in Curry, George, *David Copperfield '70*. New York, Ballantine Books, 1970.

Eliot, T. S., and Hoellering, George, *The Film of Murder in the Cathedral*. New York, Harcourt, Brace and Co., 1952.

Goldman, James, *The Lion in Winter*. New York, Random House, 1971.

Greene, Graham, and Reed, Carol, *The Third Man*. New York, Simon and Schuster, 1968.
The screenplay was entirely written by Graham Greene; Carol Reed was the director.

Manvell, Roger, ed., *Three British Screenplays: Brief Encounter, Odd Man Out, Scott of the Antarctic*. London, Methuen & Co., 1950.

Maugham, Somerset, *Encore*. Garden City, N.Y., Doubleday & Co., 1952.
Includes the screenplays by T. E. B. Clarke and others, and the original stories by Maugham from which they were adapted, for the following: *Ant and the Grasshopper, Winter Cruise,* and *Gigoloa and Gigolette.*

Maugham, Somerset, and Sherriff, R. C., *Quartet*. Garden City, N.Y., Doubleday & Co., 1949.
Includes the screenplays by Sheriff, and the stories by Maugham from which they were adapted, for the following: *Facts of Life, Alien Corn, The Kite,* and *The Colonel's Lady.*

Maugham, Somerset, *Trio*. Garden City, N.Y., Doubleday & Co., 1951.
Includes the following Maugham stories and the screenplays adapted from them: *The Verger, Mr. Know-All,* and *Sanitorium.*

Osborne, John, *Tom Jones*. New York, Grove Press, 1964.

Raphael, Frederic, *Two for the Road*. New York, Holt, Rinehart and Winston, 1967.

Shaw, George Bernard, *Pygmalion*. Baltimore, Penguin Books, 1950.

———, *Saint Joan, A Screenplay*. Seattle & London, University of Washington Press, 1968.

Thomas, Dylan, *The Doctor and the Devils, and other scripts*. New York, New Directions Publishing Corporation, 1966. Includes two screenplays: the one mentioned in the title and *Twenty Years A-Growing*.

———, *The Doctor and the Devils*. New York, New Directions Publishing Corporation, 1953.

———, *A Film Script of Twenty Years A-Growing*. London, J. M. Dent & Sons, 1964.

Watkins, Peter, *The War Game*. New York, Avon Books, 1967.

Wells, Herbert George, *The Man Who Could Work Miracles*. New York, The Macmillan Co., 1936.

Whitehead, Peter, *Wholly Communion*. London, Lorrimer Publishing, 1967.

Foreign

Antonioni, Michelangelo, *L'Avventura*, trans. by Jon Svan. New York, Grove Press, Inc., 1969. Other writers who received credit for the screenplay are Elio Bartolini and Tonio Guerra. This is, primarily, a transcription of the final film.

———, *Blow-Up*. New York, Simon and Schuster, 1971.

———, *Screenplays of Michelangelo Antonioni*, trans. by Louis Brigante and Roger J. Moore. New York, The Orion Press, 1963. Includes the following screenplays: *L'avventura, Il grido, L'eclisse*, and *La notte*.

Bellochio, Marco, and Tattoli, Elda, *China Is Near*, trans. by Judith Green. New York, The Orion Press, 1969.

Bergman, Ingmar, *Four Screenplays of Ingmar Bergman*, trans. by Lars Malmström and David Kushner. New York, Simon and Schuster, 1960. Includes the following screenplays: *Smiles of a Summer Night, The Seventh Seal, Wild Strawberries*, and *The Magician*.

———, *The Seventh Seal*, trans. by Lars Malmström and David Kushner. New York, Simon and Schuster, 1960.

———, *Three Films by Ingmar Bergman*, trans. by Paul Britten Austin. New York, Grove Press, 1970.

Includes the following screenplays: *Through a Glass Darkly, Winter Light,* and *The Silence.*

————, *Wild Strawberries,* trans. by Lars Malmström and David Kushner. New York, Simon and Schuster, 1960.
This version of Bergman's screenplay, in contrast to the one in *Four Screenplays,* contains a shot-by-shot breakdown of the entire film.

Buñuel, Luis, and Dali, Salvador, *L'Age d'or* and *Un Chien andalou,* trans. by Marianne Alexandre. New York, Simon and Schuster, 1968.

————, *Belle de Jour.* New York, Simon and Schuster, 1971.

————, *The Exterminating Angel.* New York, Simon and Schuster, 1971.

————, *Three Screenplays,* trans. by Piergiuseppe Bozzetti, Carol Martin-Sperry, and Anthony Pagden. New York, The Orion Press, Inc., 1969.
Includes the following screenplays: *Viridiana, El angel exterminador,* and *Simón del desierto.*

Carné, Marcel, *The Children of Paradise,* trans. by Dinah Brooke. New York, Simon and Schuster, 1968.
The screenplay was actually written by Jacques Prévert; Marcel Carné was the director.

Cayrol, Jean, *Night and Fog.* Included in *Film: Book 2; Films of Peace and War,* Robert Hughes, ed. New York, Grove Press, 1962.

Claire, René, *A nous la liberté* and *Entr'acte,* trans. by Nicola Hayden and Richard Jacques. New York, Simon and Schuster, 1970.

————, *Four Screenplays,* trans. by Piergiuseppe Bozzetti. New York, The Orion Press, 1970.
Includes the following screenplays: *Le Silence est d'or, La Beauté du diable, Les Belles-de-Nuit,* and *Les grandes maoeuvres.*

Cocteau, Jean, *Three Screenplays.* New York, The Viking Press, 1971.
Includes the following screenplays: *Beauty and the Beast, Orpheus,* and *Eternal Return.*

————, *Two Screenplays,* trans. by Carol Martin-Sperry. Baltimore, Penguin Books, 1969.
Includes the following screenplays: *The Blood of a Poet* and *The Testament of Orpheus.*

Dreyer, Theodore, *Four Screenplays by Theodore Dreyer,* trans. by O. Stallybrass. Bloomington and London, Indiana University Press, 1971.
Includes the following screenplays: *The Passion of Joan of Arc, Vampire, Ordet,* and *Day of Wrath.*

Duras, Marguerite, *Hiroshima mon amour,* trans. by Richard Seaver. New York, Grove Press, 1962.

———, *Une aussi longue absence,* trans. by Barbara Wright London, Calder and Boyars, 1966.
Also includes the screenplay for *Hiroshima mon amour.*

Eisenstein, Sergei M., *An American Tragedy.* Included in Montagu, Ivor, *With Eisenstein in Hollywood,* New York, International Publishers, 1969.
Also receiving credit for the script are G. V. Alexandrov and Ivor Montagu.

———, *Ivan the Terrible,* trans. by Herbert Marshall and Ivor Montagu. New York, Simon and Schuster, 1962.

———, *Old and New.* Included in Jacobs, Lewis, *Film Writing Forms.* New York, Gotham Book Mart, 1934.

———, *Potemkin,* trans. by Gillon R. Aitkin. New York, Simon and Schuster, 1968.
Also receiving credit for the screenplay is Nina Agadjhanova.

———, *Que Viva Mexico!* London, Vision Press, 1951.

———, *Sutter's Gold.* Included in Montagu, Ivor, *With Eisenstein in Hollywood.* New York, International Publishers, 1969.
Also receiving credit for the script are G. V. Alexandrov and Ivor Montagu.

———, *Fellini: Early Screenplays,* trans. by Judith Green. New York, The Orion Press, 1970.
Includes the following screenplays: *Variety Lights* and *The White Sheik.*

———, *Fellini's Satyricon,* Dario Zanelli, ed., trans. by Eugene Walter and John Matthews. New York, Ballantine Books, 1970.
Also receiving credit for the screenplay is Bernardino Zapponi.

———, *Juliet of the Spirits,* Tullio Kezich, ed., trans. by Howard Greenfield. New York, Ballantine Books, Inc., 1966. Other writers who received credit for the screenplay are Tullio Pinelli, Ennio Flaiano and Brunello Rondi. Includes the original screenplay and a transcription of the final film by John Cohen (trans. by Cecillia Perrault). Also available in hard cover from The Orion Press, New York, 1965, excepting the transcription of the final film.

————, *La dolce vita,* trans. by Oscar De Liso and Bernard Shir-Cliff. New York, Ballantine Books, 1961.
Other writers who received credit for the screenplay are Tullio Pinelli, Ennio Flaiano and Brunello Rondi.

————, *Three Screenplays,* trans. by Judith Green. New York, The Orion Press, 1970.
Includes the following screenplays: *I vitelloni, Il bidone,* and *The Temptations of Dr. Antonio.*

Godard, Jean-Luc, *Alphaville,* trans. by Peter Whitehead. New York, Simon and Schuster, 1968.

————, *Le petit soldat,* trans. by Nicholas Garnham. New York, Simon and Schuster, 1971.
This is a transcription of the final film. (NB: In my discussion of this film, I referred to the British edition of this screenplay, which is published by Lorrimer Publishing, and which is, to my knowledge, identical with the Simon and Schuster edition.)

————, *Made in USA,* trans. by Nicholas Fry. London, Lorrimer Publishing, 1967.

————, *A Married Woman,* trans. by U. Molinaro. New York, Berkeley Publishing Corporation (Medallion), 1965.

————, *Masculine-Feminine.* New York, Grove Press, 1969. This is a transcription of the final film.

————, *Pierrot le Fou,* trans. by Peter Whitehead. New York, Simon and Schuster, 1969.

————, *Weekend,* Robert Hughes, ed. New York, Grove Press, 1971.

Isaksson, Ulla, *The Virgin Spring,* trans. by Lars Malmström and David Kushner. New York, Ballantine Books, 1960.

Kurosawa, Akira, *Ikiru,* Donald Richie, ed. New York, Simon and Schuster, 1968.
Other writers who received credit for the screenplay are Shinobu Hashimoto and Hideo Oguni.

————, *Rashomon,* trans. by Donald Richie. New York, Simon and Schuster, 1969.
Also receiving credit for the screenplay is Shinobu Hashimoto. This is, principally, a transcription of the final film.

————, *Seven Samurai*. New York, Simon and Schuster, 1971.

Lang, Fritz, *M*, trans. by Nicholas Garnham. New York, Simon and Schuster, 1968.
The screenplay was actually written by Thea von Harbou; Fritz Lang was the director.

————, *Metropolis*. New York, Simon and Schuster, 1971.

Lelouch, Claude, *A Man and a Woman*. New York, Simon and Schuster, 1971.

Menzel, Jiří, *Closely Watched Trains*. New York, Simon and Schuster, 1971.

Natanson, Jacques, and Ophüls, Max, *Le Plaisir*. Included in *Sight and Sound*, London, Vol. 22, No. 1 (July–Sept., 1952).

Pabst, G. W., *Pandora's Box*. New York, Simon and Schuster, 1971.

Pasolini, Pier Paolo, *Oedipus Rex*. New York, Simon and Schuster, 1971.

Prévert, Jacques, and Carné, Marcel, *Le Jour se lève*, trans. by Dinah Brooke and Nicole Hayden. New York, Simon and Schuster, 1970.
The screenplay was actually written by Jacques Prévert and Jacques Viot; Marcel Carné was the director.

Pudovkin, V. I., *Mother*. New York, Simon and Schuster, 1971.

Renoir, Jean, *La Grande Illusion*, trans. by Marianne Alexandre and Andrew Sinclair. New York, Simon and Schuster, 1968.
Also receiving credit for the screenplay is Charles Spaak.

————, *Rules of the Game*, trans. by John McGrath and Maureen Teitelbaum. New York, Simon and Schuster, 1970.
Also receiving credit for the screenplay are Camille François, Karl Koch, and the cast.

Robbe-Grillet, Alain, *Last Year at Marienbad*, trans. by Richard Howard. New York, Grove Press, 1962.

Semprun, Jorge, *La Guerre est finie*, trans. by Richard Seaver. New York, Grove Press, 1967.

Sica, Vittorio De, *The Bicycle Thief*, trans. by Simon Hartog. New York, Simon and Schuster, 1968.
The following writers also received credit for the screenplay: Cesare Zavattini, Oreste Biancoli, Adolfo Franci, Gherardo Gherardi, Gerardo Guerrieri, and Suso Cecchi D'Amico.

————, *Miracle in Milan*. Baltimore, Penguin Books, 1969.
The following writers also received credit for the screenplay:

Cesare Zavattini, Suso Cecchi D'Amico, Mario Chiari, and Adolfo Franci.

Sontag, Susan, *Duet for Cannibals*. New York, Farrar, Straus and Giroux, 1969.

Teshigahara, Hiroshi, *Woman in the Dunes*. New York, Phaedra Publishers, 1966.

Truffaut, François, *The Four Hundred Blows*, David Denby, ed., trans. by David Denby and Henry F. Mins. New York, Grove Press, 1969.
Also receiving credit for the screenplay is Marcel Moussy. This is, principally, a transcription of the final film.

————, *Jules and Jim*, trans. by Nicholas Fry. New York, Simon and Schuster, 1968.
Also receiving credit for the screenplay is Jean Grunault.

Vadim, Roger; Brulé, Claude; and Vailland, Roger; *Les Liaisons dangereuses*, trans. by Bernard Shir-Cliff. New York, Ballantine Books, Inc., 1962.

Visconti, Luchino, *Three Screenplays*, trans. by Judith Green. New York, The Orion Press, 1970.
Includes the following screenplays: *White Nights, Rocco and His Brothers,* and *The Job*.

————, *Two Screenplays*, trans. by Judith Green. New York, The Orion Press, 1970.
Includes the following screenplays: *La terra trema* and *Senso*.

von Sternberg, Josef, *The Blue Angel*. New York, Simon and Schuster, 1968.
This is a transcription of the final film.

Welles, Orson, *The Trial*. New York, Simon and Schuster, 1971.
This is a transcription of the final film.

Wiene, Robert, *The Cabinet of Dr. Caligari*. New York, Simon and Schuster, 1971.

Appendix C
Information on Film Rentals

Those readers interested in renting 16mm prints of the films discussed in this book for college classroom or film society showing should consult *Feature Films on 8mm and 16mm*, 3rd ed., compiled and edited by James L. Limbacher (New York, R. R. Bowker Co., 1971), for the names and addresses of the nearest distributors. For changes in distributors and additional listings for the aforementioned source, the reader should consult the bi-monthly periodical *Sightlines*, published by the Educational Film Library Association, 17 West 60th Street, New York, N.Y. 10023.

The reader will find many of the shorter Underground films mentioned in this book which are not listed in the above-mentioned sources listed in the catalogue of the Film-Makers's Co-operative, 175 Lexington Avenue, New York, N.Y. 10016.

Index

WIDENER COLLEGE
WOLFGRAM LIBRARY
CHESTER, PA.